DEREK WALCOTT

WALKER AND THE GHOST DANCE

Derek Walcott was born in St. Lucia in 1930. His *Collected Poems: 1948–1984* was published in 1986, and his subsequent works include a book-length poem, *Omeros* (1990); a collection of verse, *The Bounty* (1997); and, in an edition illustrated with his own paintings, the long poem *Tiepolo's Hound* (2000). His most recent collection of plays is *The Haitian Trilogy* (2001). He received the Nobel Prize in Literature in 1992.

ALSO BY DEREK WALCOTT

POEMS

Selected Poems

The Gulf

Another Life

Sea Grapes

The Star-Apple Kingdom

The Fortunate Traveller

Midsummer

Collected Poems: 1948–1984

The Arkansas Testament

Omeros

The Bounty

Tiepolo's Hound

PLAYS

Dream on Monkey Mountain and Other Plays

The Joker of Seville and O Babylon!

Remembrance and Pantomime

Three Plays: The Last Carnival; Beef, No Chicken;

Branch of the Blue Nile

The Odyssey

The Haitian Trilogy

ESSAYS

What the Twilight Says

WALKER

AND

THE GHOST DANCE

WALKER

AND

THE GHOST DANCE

·

DEREK WALCOTT

·

FARRAR, STRAUS AND GIROUX

NEW YORK

Farrar, Straus and Giroux

19 Union Square West, New York 10003

Copyright © 2002 by Derek Walcott

All rights reserved

Distributed in Canada by Douglas & McIntyre Ltd.

Printed in the United States of America

First edition, 2002

ISBN: *0-374-52814-4*

Library of Congress Control Number: 2002101069

Designed by Abby Kagan

www.fsgbooks.com

1   3   5   7   9   10   8   6   4   2

CONTENTS

Foreword   *vii*

Walker   *1*

The Ghost Dance   *115*

FOREWORD

Both of these plays originated as commissions, both are completely American in history and setting, and both deal with disenfranchisement and deprivation.

The Boston Athenaeum commissioned the libretto of *Walker* for an opera by T. J. Anderson, which I revised as a play with music by Galt MacDermot.

The Ghost Dance had as its model a John Ford film with its usual stock characters—an Irish sergeant, a tough independent widow—and its standard setting of a fort. For fluency the staging should have little furniture; drapes, flags, and blankets could be used for scene changes.

D.W.

New York, 2002

WALKER

·

In memory of Romare Bearden

I see them walking in a cloud of glory
Whose light doth trample on my days.
—HENRY VAUGHAN

Walker was produced by the Boston Athenaeum as an opera by T. J. Anderson with libretto by Derek Walcott for one performance only, on December 9, 1993. It was directed by Donna Roll. Featured singers were:

WALKER—*Robert Honeysucker*
ELIZABETH—*Andrea Bradford*
    With *Frank Ragsdale, Elisabeth Borg, Matthew Molloy,* and *Vincent Stringer*

A rewritten version of *Walker*, with music by Galt MacDermot, was produced by the Boston Playwrights Theatre in November 2001. It was directed by Wesley Savick, with set design by Richard Chambers. The cast was as follows:

DAVID WALKER—*Jonathan Earl Peck*
ELIZA WALKER—*Merle Perkins*
THE FIGURE—*Will Lyman*
WILLIAM LLOYD GARRISON—*Edwin McDonough*
CATHERINE HEALEY—*Stacy Rock*
BARBADOS—*J. Bernard Calloway*
CHORUS—*Stephanie Marson Lee, Andrea Lyman, Gamalia Pharms, Kathryn Woods*

CAST OF CHARACTERS
(IN ORDER OF APPEARANCE)

A FIGURE, *white, fifties, Southern*

WILLIAM LLOYD GARRISON, *Irish*

ELIZA WALKER, *David Walker's wife, black, late twenties, Southern*

DAVID WALKER, *black, aged forty-five, Southern*

CATHERINE HEALEY, *Irish, early twenties*

BARBADOS, *black, ex-slave, thirties*

CHORUS

PLACE: *Boston, 1830*

TIME: *The action takes place on Brattle Street on the last Thanksgiving Day of David Walker's life.*

Brattle Street. Walker's house. Thanksgiving. Early snow. A
FIGURE *in a long black coat waits under a streetlamp.*
GARRISON *is going towards the house.*

FIGURE

Sir! Forgive me.

GARRISON

Yes?

FIGURE

Is that David Walker's house?

GARRISON

It is.

(*The* FIGURE *walks up to the window, then returns to*
GARRISON.)

FIGURE

And that machine is the press?

GARRISON

Yes.

FIGURE

That now does the work of the devil.
Keep the niggers from printing machines.
Deliver us from that evil.

GARRISON

I don't quite know what that means.

FIGURE

Sir, I stand here swaying with hunger
because of my brotherhood's vow.
I won't eat until I see that nigger
spread-eagled in the snow.
I'm as starved as a crow in winter
cawing on a field-fence,

keeping its keen yellow eye
on all who leave and enter.
I've learnt to wait quietly
until what must happen, happens.

(*The* FIGURE *waits in the shadows;* GARRISON
approaches it.)

GARRISON

Come into the light,
this damned street's cold and dark.

FIGURE

No. The light is too late.
Too late to do business.

GARRISON

What business? What business?

FIGURE

You're asking me a lot.
The pamphlet must not be printed.

GARRISON

Whom do you represent, sir?
(*Pause*)
Sir, whom do you represent?

FIGURE

You insist on an answer?
I go where I am sent.
Unless you want him dead,
the pamphlet must not be printed.

GARRISON

You've got a Southern accent.
Are you from where, Georgia?

FIGURE

Mr. Garrison, I can change my accent
if it'd make you happier.

GARRISON

You know damned well why I ask.

FIGURE

Why?

GARRISON

        There're certain men from Georgia
who're out to skin his hide,
who've put out a reward, sir,
to capture or have him killed.
If you're not their representative
who want him dead or alive

out here in this freezing cold,
leave the darkness, for the light.
Come with me, come inside.
Don't stand there like a raven
in the afternoon snow,
or a black crow in the cotton.
Come into his house, now.

FIGURE

And, you, don't come any closer;
don't leave the light you're in.
I've got a pistol, a revolver
that could send you spinning
right here in the fresh snow.
I am not from a Southern state, sir,
I represent a state.
The fact is, I'm a senator
and my republic is . . .

GARRISON

What?

FIGURE

Death.

GARRISON

I'm going to call the police.

FIGURE

What is the charge?

GARRISON

Loitering with intent.
To murder. You are an assassin.

FIGURE

Necessity is my only sin.
I am as white as the snow, sir,
and, Mr. Garrison, as innocent.
I'll be gone when it stops snowing.

GARRISON

Nevertheless I'm going.
(*The* FIGURE *stumbles, staggers, collapses to his knees on the
snow.*)
What's wrong?

(*The* FIGURE *draws his pistol.*)

FIGURE

Stay back! It'll pass; it'll pass.
It was the smell of food.
The smell of Thanksgiving.

GARRISON

Do you need help? Do you need to lie down?

FIGURE

No. No. It goes. It comes in waves.

I have not eaten for four days.

When he dies, my fast will be broken.

Then I can resume living.

(*He rises to his feet, swaying.*)

GARRISON

I'm going to have you arrested.

Arrested, sir! Do you hear?

FIGURE

Go! I know how to disappear.

You call the police, sir.

(*He puts the pistol away, walks backwards into the dark. As he exits*)

By the time they get here,

I'll be invisible.

I'll be white air.

(GARRISON *runs into the dark alley, searching and shouting.*)

GARRISON

You can't stop us!

If you come back, the police!

(*He runs towards the house, pounds on the door. The door is locked tight. He rattles the doorknob, looks at the upstairs window.*)

David! David! Open up!

David, it's William Garrison.

(*To himself*)

There's a lamp in the upstairs window.

Eliza! Are you in there?

I'm out here in the damned snow.

Listen. I've gone to fetch the . . .

(*To himself*)

No. Better if they didn't know.

If you can hear me, Eliza,

don't open to anyone else.

I have to go to the police

about a certain business.

Keep this door locked now.

Tell David I have some news.

(*He hurries across the street through the piled drifts. Behind the curtains we see a lamp descend the stairs and come to a downstairs window. A woman, ELIZA, parts the curtains and looks out. The FIGURE is there, under the streetlamp; then the FIGURE steps back into the alley. We enter the parlour of the house. It is also the store where* WALKER *sells used clothes from racks. There is a small counter and a hand-operated printing press with a table with paper and typefaces.* ELIZA *enters with a lamp.*)

ELIZA (*To herself*)

Oh, David, David, come inside.
    (WALKER *enters, carrying kindling; he places it by the hearth.*)
Where were you? Where've you been?

WALKER

In the back yard to fetch some kindling.

ELIZA

Good. To light the fire in the hearth
as well as our hearts, David.
Today is Thanksgiving.

WALKER

What are we giving thanks for?

ELIZA

For being alive. For freedom.
For being able to see our breath still.
    (*She returns to the window.*)

WALKER

What you keep on looking out for?

Is there something you scared of?

ELIZA

Today carries a terrible fear.

I thought I saw something move.

Am I seeing things? I don't know.

I thought I saw something just now,

like a raven walking in the snow.

Like a black crow hopping in the cotton;

but it goes every time I turn.

I can't see his colour, his face,

but it been walking round and round

like a buzzard, circling this place,

and the snow don't make no sound.

WALKER

This ain't the South, Liza, please.

ELIZA

Is he still there? Can you see him?

(WALKER *goes to the window. Sees him. Lies.*)

WALKER

No.

ELIZA

He walks with that slow rhythm
of a crow walking carefully.

WALKER

    I'm sick of this thing.
I see only snow blowing, white air.
It's a blizzard, not a buzzard out there;
it's snowing and the street is dim,
and you see strange shadows in winter.
Come on, you just had a bad dream.

ELIZA

I see you lying on the white ground.
That's the dream I have, David.

WALKER

And you go be my Bathsheba?

ELIZA

No, I'm Eliza, your wife.
But, David, I know what the name mean,
and the name go fit your life.

WALKER

Boy-killer of Goliath, David.
And you ain't go be my Bathsheba?

ELIZA

David, I'm Eliza, your wife!

WALKER

David, the harp-player. David, the king!

ELIZA

Whose harp got only one string
and who got to keep harping, harping
that what ain't right is wrong.

WALKER

David, the giant-slayer.
Liza, my head's getting grayer.
I'm not no stripling no more.
Maybe I'm David, the nay-sayer,
but possession is nine-tenths of the law,
and the law can't prevent our dreams.

ELIZA

I been here since dawn whitened the window
and wondering where you were just now,
what you was dreaming, and I get so frighten
of today, Lord, I don't know.
You got to tell me your dream.

WALKER

(WALKER *crosses to the printer, cranks its arm into position, then stops.*)

WALKER

I was walking alone through a forest
of black trees whose leaves were like print,
but their language was different
and the leaves were letters I had learnt
but forgotten, from the African kingdoms,
and I was both lost and not lost.
And all of the leaves were talking,
in tongues I almost understood,
and I, David Walker, kept walking
as if towards my own ghost,
through these letters in a dark wood.
I was remembering an alphabet
from a language I did not know,
then I looked outside the window
and the drums no longer beat,
and saw Boston smothered in snow
and the snow blurring Brattle Street,
and bare trees like dark iron, and wet.
But it's easy to explain the dream now;
it's because of the hard work I do,
setting type, changing this pamphlet
that I'm reprinting tomorrow.

But you asked me, and I tell you
something I'd rather forget.

ELIZA

Gonna confess, confess
to something you won't understand,
you and that damned printing press,
and I never thought I'd say this:
I miss the land.

WALKER

Where, what land, Africa?
Because, Liza, that is our true land.

ELIZA

Which Africa? Whose Africa?
I don't know no Africa.
I ain't going and I never been there.
Something's changed in you, David;
you're tight, you no longer hear,
you so caught up in this press.
It's the only sound in your head.

WALKER

Which land? I'm sorry, Eliza.

ELIZA

I miss it, deep, and it hurt.
Not Beulah Land, but red dirt.

WALKER

Come on, North Carolina?

ELIZA

Yes.

WALKER

You going crazy, you hear?

ELIZA

The tall green pines. And blood red dirt.
Maybe I'm just tired of the snow,
maybe I'll never get used to winter,
but I wish, this Thanksgiving,
with the bells muffled in cotton,
I wish I was back there now.

WALKER

Know what you sound like? A mule,
an old mule longing for the plough.
Come on, woman, don't be a fool.
Miss Carolina? The cotton
and the niggers bending low?

ELIZA

I knew you'd say that. I know
that that past should be forgotten,
but that's the earth where I was born.
I just miss it, maybe I just miss our courtin'
days, but I miss it, and my heart is torn.

(*She goes to another window.*)

It's like a burst goosedown pillow.
That silent, merciless snow.
I wish it was the shreds
of your damned declaration
that you insist on printing.
God save me for saying this now,
but better we had stayed ignorant
than fallen for the temptation
of bettering our minds.
Know what the snow does? It blinds.
It blinds us with whiteness,
until everything we see
is white, and it hides the truth.
But back in Carolina,
as illiterate as we was,
we smelt the pines and the earth,
we knew exacterly,
without their books and promises,
exacterly what we was worth.

WALKER

Say "exactly."

ELIZA

Say what?

WALKER

Say "exactly"!

ELIZA

Exacterly what?

WALKER

The word is not "exacterly."
The word is "ex-act-ly." Say it.

ELIZA

You say it.

WALKER

SAY IT! SAY IT!
SAY IT, GODDAMNIT. SAY IT, LIZA.

ELIZA

Go to Hell, David!

WALKER

I'll wait for you there.

ELIZA

For what sin?

WALKER

Stubbornness.

ELIZA

You set me the example.

(*Pause.*)

WALKER

Exactly.
(*She cries. He embraces her.*)
Come on, Eliza, laugh.

ELIZA

Laugh? 'Bout what?

WALKER

Smile, then, turn the sunshine on,
and you know what will happen after that,
that street outside go be Carolina cotton;
smile, big as the country, wide as prairie wheat.

ELIZA

I ain't smilin', David Walker, go on.

WALKER (*Sings.*)

Don't want to see no head-scarfed sobbin' woman,
Don't want no sad woman for my wife,
Don't want to watch no frown like some storm comin'
'Cross a Carolina cotton field all my life.

Don't need to hear no grumblin' and no moaning,
Or watch no faraway thunder drum your brow,
Don't want you wakin' mis'rable in the morning,
Tired as a mule that's harnessed to a plough.

Don't want no passing sorrow to remind her.
I want to see our early courtin' days,
Want a springtime sunrise in North Carolina,
Want the larks of heaven rising in her praise.

Time know she got no reason to be grinnin',
Though winter's here and winter sunshine's thin,
But don't want to see no head-scarfed sobbin' woman,
'Cause I love her even more than I did then.

(WALKER *and* ELIZA *go to the rack of clothes and put on*
hats, heavy coats. The CHORUS *now visible.*)

CHORUS

Romare Bearden, bear our burden,
Horace Pippin, paint our pain.

Keep our innocence, Jacob Lawrence,
Deep in the American grain.

(WALKER *and* ELIZA *and* FRIENDS, *with baggage, leaving*
North Carolina. ELIZA *turns to look,* WALKER *turns her*
around. Projections: Bearden, Pippin, Lawrence.)

WALKER (*Sings.*)

Don't look behind us, Liza,
Like Lot's wife in Gomorrah;
Before us is the future,
Behind us is our sorrow.
Don't look behind, like Lot's wife;
She turned into a white pillar of salt,
A snow-woman in the snow.
We cannot change their fault.

ELIZA

We're going to a safer place;
Behind us is our yesterdays.
There's a beacon up there shining
On a hill in Boston.

I won't look behind me pining,
Or I'll turn to a pillar of salt.
Leave the fields of snowy cotton,
We're gone, we're gone.
Carolina'll be forgotten,
Our bondage is our fault.

CHORUS

Keep our innocence, Jacob Lawrence,
Horace Pippin, paint our pain.

Romare Bearden, bear our burden,
Deep in the American grain.

WALKER

I see a city on a hill,
Its walls as white as snow.
Deliver us from evil:
The red earth and the plough.

CHORUS

Romare Bearden, bear our burden,
Horace Pippin, paint our pain.

Keep our innocence, Jacob Lawrence,
Frederick Douglass, lift your pen.

(CHORUS exits. *Live collages: Carolina pastoral. Romare Bearden, Jacob Lawrence, Horace Pippin. Rural scenes, black.* ELIZA *and* WALKER *replace their costumes. A heavy pounding on the door.*
GARRISON *knocks on the door.*)

ELIZA

Who's pounding on the door?
Who's that knocking?

(WALKER *peeps through the curtains.*)

WALKER

It's Garrison. Tell him I'm out.
I don't . . . I'm not ready to see him.

(*He goes out through the back door.* ELIZA *lets* GARRISON *in.*)

ELIZA

Happy Thanksgiving, Mr. Garrison.
Last year we ate together.
I would invite you to eat with us,
but David's forbidden any celebration.
He says we have nothing to be thankful for.
That we can't celebrate our freedom.
He says niggers have the freedom of turkeys.

(*Laughs.*)

You're welcome to whatever we have.

David owes you everything.

GARRISON

I love the man, Liza. You know that.

I'm deeply indebted, Liza,

but I'll be needed back at my own house.

(*He goes to the press.*)

I see the type is all set

and he's ready to reprint.

ELIZA

He worked on it all night.

GARRISON

The pamphlet. He should wait.

(*He goes to the window. No one in the street or under the lamp.*)

There's no one under the streetlight.

ELIZA

What?

GARRISON

David should not go out into the street.

ELIZA

He's in the yard cutting kindling.
He loves the axe biting into wood.
He'll be in in a while. Won't you sit?

(GARRISON *sits.*)

GARRISON

So how are you, Mistress Eliza?
The snow is astonishingly early this year.

ELIZA

Oh, Mr. Garrison, I'm so full of dread.
This coming Boston winter.
Cold black iron and fresh blue snow
on the cold black iron, on the brick
of the snooty high houses, and the sky
soggy as a soaked blanket.
                    (*She shudders.*)

GARRISON

I understand how you must miss the South.
But if David left Boston to follow the sun,
you do not have to guess the consequences.

ELIZA

He'd be shot down in his flight like a wild duck.

GARRISON

And that's the risk. Where is he?

(*He goes to the window, parts the drapes, draws them tight.*)

ELIZA

He should be in Gilead,

but he's still here. He's fetching firewood

from out in the back yard.

(GARRISON *rushes towards the back door and meets* WALKER

entering, snow-powdered, carrying some logs.)

GARRISON

David: Oh thank God!

WALKER

For what?

GARRISON

For firelight, for safety, for a good Thanksgiving dinner.

For your being warm and safe.

(WALKER *rests the logs down near the hearth, dusts himself off.*)

Mother of God, I'm thirsty.

I'd kill for a drop of whisky.

WALKER

Excuse us, Liza. She's got a prayer meeting.

(ELIZA *leaves.*)

GARRISON

Where's the drink? I see you've gone ahead
and set up the type for the pamphlet.

WALKER

I can't drink with you. Not yet.

(WALKER *brings a decanter of whisky and one glass. He*
pauses. GARRISON *pours his own drink.*)

GARRISON

David, what's wrong?

WALKER

There is a deep division.

GARRISON

I know, I have come a bit early.

WALKER

No, you haven't come too early,
Mr. Garrison, you've come too late.

GARRISON

Too late? Too late for what?

WALKER

There is a deep division.
A deep trench, Mr. Garrison.

GARRISON

What's this Mr. Garrison business?

WALKER

A permanent decision.
             (*He extends his arms over the press.*)
Behold me, William Garrison,
crucified on my printing press.
There is our final division.

GARRISON

Division between us, David?
Ah, not between us, surely.
What is this Mr. Garrison,
David, Bill Garrison, your friend?

WALKER

There is a deep division
between us, William Garrison,
and that's how it must end.
A deep and sad decision.
Drink. And we must not argue.

GARRISON

Drink, said the Centurion

piercing Him with the spear,

then the sponge of vinegar.

(*Drinks.*)

Is it something that I said,

that our friendship is murdered

without any of my defence?

Was it something I uttered,

something of mine you read

and possibly misinterpreted

and utterly misunderstood?

WALKER

There stands William Garrison,

abolitionist editor,

model, Solon, mentor;

but this is not David Walker

that is the deep division

that has finally come to pass

between me and William Garrison,

a friendship drained, but no more

than the air in an empty glass.

(*Silence.*)

GARRISON

There is now a price on your head,
A ten-thousand-dollar reward
from a group of Georgia men
known as the Brotherhood
who have vowed to fast unto death
until they have seen or heard
of the whisper of your last breath,
David, like the snow outside.
One thousand dollars for you dead,
Ten thousand for you alive.

(*Silence.*)

David!

WALKER

Are you sorry you taught me to read?

GARRISON

Damn it, David, what do you mean?

WALKER

Or jealous that I can now write?

GARRISON

I am someone you used to love.

WALKER

Let my murderer be the word.

(*He picks up a piece of type.*)

GARRISON

There're people who'll want this reward.

WALKER

If that happens, look after my wife.

(*He replaces the piece of type.*)

GARRISON

Where is this new arrogance from?

WALKER

What arrogance, Mr. Garrison?

GARRISON

What arrogance? This one.

WALKER

Are you talking about natural pride?

GARRISON

No, this air of walking to your doom.

This new joy in martyrdom,

and not martyrdom, suicide.

(*He lifts out his own piece of type.*)
Don't reprint this. Not this pamphlet.
No more pamphlets like this, no more;
it's not only the Congress, the Senate,
but a gathering avalanche,
a blizzard of voices will answer you
in a white, terrible roar.

(WALKER *takes the type piece from* GARRISON *and
replaces it.*)

WALKER

It'll be out on the streets tomorrow.

GARRISON

Predecessors and exemplars
have fired me on:
Judge Samuel Sewall's pleas
against slavery in Boston,
and also on your side, David;
we are not in all this alone.

WALKER

Since I moved from City Market
to this, 27 Brattle Street.
Abhor my direction, attack it,
but I have always walked straight.

I am tired of patience,
of your New England society,
your measured abolitionists;
your friends ain't no longer my friends.

GARRISON

You owe me your friendship.

(WALKER *lifts up a whisky glass with exaggerated flair.*)

WALKER

I owe you a lot. My manners, too.
I almost fell into that amiable trap
of being escorted and introduced
to the brandy and firelight of Beacon Hill,
to the pink and liberal warmth
of Boston society, until I saw
where all that near affection was heading:
into conspicuous tolerance, into the pride
your good friends took in being good to me.
Oh, you meant well, no doubt, but I felt awkward.
I could have fitted in quite easily,
since abolition was the fashionable thing,
but I withdrew, as you remember.

GARRISON

I remember.

WALKER

So from that to this was easy.
Wouldn't you say?

GARRISON

Perhaps.

WALKER

Not only easy
but inevitable.

GARRISON

There I disagree.

WALKER

And here, you and I part company.

GARRISON

David, you've got to leave now.

WALKER

Why?

GARRISON

There's a fellow out there all set to murder you.

WALKER

It's Thanksgiving. Let me invite him in.

(*He moves to the door.* GARRISON *blocks his steps.*)

GARRISON

I went to the police. They can do nothing
unless there is a violation, a specific charge;
not against someone strolling in the street.
In other words, when you die I can complain.
Otherwise it's just blind snow and justice.
But suspicion is insufficient.
Besides, they know who you are and what you do.
They won't exactly rush to save you.
Leave here with Eliza. Shelter in my home.

WALKER

As the coon said to the hound:
"I'm tired o' running."

(GARRISON *collapses into a chair.*)

GARRISON

God forgive me. I brought this on you.

WALKER

Go home, Mr. Garrison. Bill.

(GARRISON *looks up at the momentary tenderness.*)
Home to your family.

GARRISON

Join us. I'll leave if you'll join us.
                    (*He waits. Silence.*)
So you're going to do nothing?

WALKER

What can I do? I can't alter my fate.

GARRISON

And now I could even think you sent for him
to make a certainty of your martyrdom.
Otherwise, why can't you leave this house
and hide in places where we'd find you shelter,
even another country? And do it now!
I have friends in England, abolitionists.
Change into some old clothes, disguise yourself.
Here, let me help you choose something. This, or this.
       (*He searches the rack of clothes.* WALKER *bars him.*)
No. Not you! There isn't a coat in here
to suit your arrogance.

WALKER

I was born a free man, I inherited it
from my mother, 'cause that was your law,

on my mother's side. I knew the spirit
of freedom, my father—well, that was another
side, the slave side. I'm no longer split.
I can't split myself from my brother.

GARRISON

The great black orator
Samuel Snowden . . .

WALKER

Samuel Snowden. White nigger.

GARRISON

The great orator Samuel Snowden
we all take pride in.
Bred out of Boston.
Crispus Attucks, emancipator.
Add your own name to theirs.

WALKER

But I ain't a true citizen,
and perhaps there is a wide
difference in between
your own city, outside,
and my own city, within;
the inner city, no pride,
no shame, just weariness,

weariness and resignation,
and that's the city I know,
and forever more I can see.
You want patience from every Negro,
like a snail. Go slow, go slow.

GARRISON

No, there is a greater acceleration
to our common goal than you think.
Oh, for God's sake, David, give in.
My tongue's blue for another drink.

(*He pours himself a huge whisky.*)

WALKER

Not progress, but self-deceit,
the illusion of progress,
no more crawlin', our own two feet.
Would you spend an entire day
watching a horned, crawlin' snail
moving inches by labourin' inches
towards its dim destination?
Well, that's how this whole nation
studies our African progress.

GARRISON

Your choice is violence.

WALKER

Yes.

(*Pause.*)

A calculated friendship,

that's all that ours was.

(GARRISON *slowly withdraws a pistol.*)

GARRISON

I went back home after that stranger

to a scene of quiet consternation

from my wife and my children and friends,

waiting and worried. I brought you this pistol.

Take it. If this is how it ends.

(*He offers* WALKER *the pistol.* WALKER *turns his back to
him.* GARRISON *rests the pistol near the press.*)

I'll leave it here. Close to the press.

It's your right as a citizen.

WALKER

Do you mean I can shoot white people?

GARRISON

Yes. You have my permission.

WALKER

To massacre?

GARRISON

No, to kill—one. Me.

(*Despite themselves they laugh.*)

Embrace me, David, dear friend.

(*Silence.*)

WALKER

I write not for you but my brothers.

That's something they don't see.

GARRISON

And do you know what they'll attest?

This savage preaches murder

as justice, the evildoer

as a horror justified.

WALKER

Rage will restore our pride.

GARRISON

Don't reprint it.

Don't reprint it.

You attract your own murder,

the opportunity of equal hate.

This is sedition. I have heard the

reaction, and right now you hear it.

This is sedition, not debate.
It was circulated in the Senate.
In the swirls of this whispering snow
white voices are rising against it,
and a figure is stalking you now.

WALKER

I have seen it crossing the window.
For one minute I thought it was you.

(He goes to the door, opens it.)

GARRISON

Want to go back where you're from?
A snail crawling back to Wilmington
in North Carolina,
to the plough, the shack, and the mule,
and the white, foaming cotton.
Has the snail forgotten,
when it got here it couldn't read,
its horns were blind as fingers
tracing words on a page:
and do you think a blizzard cares
for what is only a snail's rage?

WALKER

The snail taught itself to read
by crawlin', feelerin' out each word,

but it owes you no gratitude.
The snail read about hatred
when inside the snail there was none;
all that the poor snail remembered
was the North Carolina sun.
Well, the snail's turned to a man now,
the mule's turned loose from the plough.
Goodbye, Bill Garrison.

GARRISON

Publish and perish, then.
This just came over the wire.
Print your own execution,
it has happened before in Boston.
The actions of the legislature—
this is an out-and-out war—
Virginia's, Mississippi's,
North Carolina's, Georgia's,
Louisiana's published these decrees
to make it a capital offence
to incite any servile attempts
at insurrection; that's why I came here,
to prevent your own murder,
although you advocate here
the slaughter of my own kind.
Prison and a heavy fine
await those who, including the wind,

circulate such literature.
Do not open your door.

(WALKER *goes to the press, begins to print the pamphlet.*
GARRISON *exits. The* FIGURE *appears under the streetlamp.*
GARRISON *walks past him, head down in the loud, strong*
wind.)

SCENE TWO

A half hour later. CATHERINE, *a cleaning girl, is fitting on*
an apron, setting plates in a corner. WALKER *is setting type.*

WALKER

Finished the housecleaning?

CATHERINE

Yes, Mr. Walker.

WALKER

What else have you to do?

CATHERINE
Set the table,
put away some kitchenware, baste the turkey.

WALKER
You see what I'm doing, don't you, Catherine?

CATHERINE
Yes, sir.

WALKER
And what's that exactly?

CATHERINE
You still setting those letters,
those little pieces of lead, you said,
in their proper place, reversed,
so that when you pull the paper,
it prints itself sensibly.

(WALKER *leads her to the bed of the printing press.*)

WALKER
Can you try to read it, Catherine?
Can you tell me what this letter is?
(*He holds up a letter.*)

CATHERINE

Is it a G, sir?

WALKER

A G turned backwards, God.
Would you like me to set out your name
and print it, Catherine Healey?

CATHERINE

I should finish my work, Mr. Walker.
Miss Eliza'll be back from the meetinghouse.
She'd like here spick and shining.

WALKER

Catherine, aren't you curious?
That's why you keep your innocence.
You've no curiosity, have you?
When Miss ransomed you from the workhouse,
she valued that quality most.
But, Catherine, you should be curious.

CATHERINE

I've no proper education.
I never had time for one,
not if you're an orphan.
Life went down another road.
A country road in Ireland,

then a rough ship to Boston.
Sir, you taught yourself to read?

WALKER

Catherine, all it takes is determination.
When I began I saw the thick page as a forest
with no track to go through, excepting my own will,
and the determination in my fear.
The white page was black with trees; what I did first
was study each tree, its shape, syllable by syllable,
letter by letter, leaf by leaf, and I learnt by myself
what the leaf symbols were; I said the sound for each leaf,
till I could comprehend each tree,
then the whole tree, till the tree was one sound,
over leaves that fell onto the ground,
and as I went deeper in the page, in the rhythm
of my walking, passing under sentences,
ducking my head under them,
I could see a light far ahead
and I wanted to read a book.
I moved slowly, slowly, with the rage of a snail
to get damned well where it was headed,
and I took down this Bible

(*He shows her a Bible.*)

from the first page, which is:
In the beginning was the Word.
I read it, Catherine. I read it!

There: Come on, girl. Don't look so defeated.

In the beginning was the Word. Read.

CATHERINE

Oh no, sir, no, sir, it's too late.

What would I do with such an education,

and me just your scullery maid?

(*Knocking on the door.* WALKER *takes up* GARRISON's *pistol,*

goes to the door, opens it. Nothing. A gust of wind blows

some snow in.)

Who was it, sir? Who knocked?

WALKER

Nobody. There's nothing in the street.

Maybe a loose door was banging, or a window.

(*He fastens the door, puts the pistol back, near the press.*)

CATHERINE

Is there any trouble, sir?

WALKER

Yes. I forgot to tell you.

It comes with the reading.

But you're not in any danger.

(*He starts the printing press, its rhythm under.*)

Next I'll teach you this skill,

of how this machine prints

your thought; it is a great talker.
Now I can print my own forest
of thoughts on this page,
circulate it, in this abolitionist
and seditious rag.

   (*He holds up a printed pamphlet, stops the press.*)

CATHERINE

What is it this pamphlet says?

WALKER

I'll show you another pamphlet.
     (*He gets another pamphlet.*)

CATHERINE

Don't try to make me read it, sir;
the letters get me tired. I need a rest.

WALKER

This is not my pamphlet, it's theirs.
1641, the citizens of Massachusetts.
Follow the snail with its feelers
as it crawls over the letters.

   (*He makes her hand trace the letters.*)
Appeal in Four Articles together with a Pre-Amble to the Colored Citizens of the World, but in particular and very expressly, to those of the United States of America. (*Reads.*)

There shall never be any bond slavery, villenage, or captivity
among us unless it be lawful captives taken in just wars and
such strangers as willingly sell themselves or are sold to us.
And these shall have all the liberties and Christian usages
which the laws of God require . . . This exempts none from
servitude who shall be judged thereto by authority.

Lies, subtle treacheries
here, right here in your hand,
right hand and left hand
in opposite contradiction.
This is a contract, a fiction;
on the one hand it condemns,
on the other hand it saves;
it abhors slavery, but lets them
keep slaves who have slaves;
and of course it speaks of God.
Here is the contract of evil
in the mockery of the Good.
And this one, this is my reply:

      (*He shows her the type on the bed of the press.*)

this fury for our redress,
this refusal of a white lie
that damns their God with the rest.
This pamphlet is my reply,
this my own address.

CATHERINE

Damns God, sir? I'll go to Hell
for listening to this.

WALKER

You are beaten by a Bible
back to an ignorant wilderness.

(*He grasps her wrist.*)

CATHERINE

No, no. I'll shut my ears, please.
I'll run out into the snow.

(*She covers her ears, kneels.*)

WALKER

Get up off your knees.
That's where they want us, Catherine,
they want us down there.

(*He releases her.*)

CATHERINE

This is the devil that I'm hearing.
Please, Mr. Walker, please,
no more blasphemy, no more swearing
against God, sir.

WALKER

Then stay on your knees.
You're Irish. Pray. That's what they expect,
our conquerors, Catherine.

CATHERINE

In just listening I have sinned.
I need absolution.

WALKER

There is another truth.
And killing is its solution.

CATHERINE

Killing, sir, killing what?

WALKER

Not just ideas of revolution
but the revolution itself;
first we put the Word, the Bible,
back up on its shelf
                    (*He replaces the Bible.*)
and we keep printing this pamphlet,
this engine of the truth,
and killing what?—It's not too late,
everything that is white?

CATHERINE

Killing me, sir? Killing me?

WALKER

No, all who are our oppressors,
who want to stop my addresses
and wreck our printing presses.
The one answer is in slaughter,
then they will believe our rage
till the charred forest stands
like burnt niggers on this page,
and the forest in my hands
keeps advocating the slaughter
of white people, as easy as
you drink a glass of water.
That's what God understands,
Catherine, that's what all oppressors
respect; mutual violence.
Not you, not you, Catherine.
Let those be my sins
not yours. We'll always be friends.

(CATHERINE *is sobbing.* WALKER *embraces her.*
Makes her sit.)

Listen to me gently, Catherine.

(*Pause. He is in tears.*)

When the slave bell summons the nigger
every Sunday from its steeple,

and up to the pulpit the Figure
of God rises to perpetuate this disease
of servitude and fear,
of damnation with this gibberish,
woman, Irish woman, Irish
people, cross yourself on your knees,
and whine your way to Heaven,
for the word of God is given,
and the word of God is British.

CATHERINE

Sir, cursing God is wrong.
Otherwise, sir, I am leaving.

(ELIZA *enters.*)

ELIZA

Well, it's cold as the grave in here.
(*The door swings open.*)
God, girl, did you leave the door open?
(*She shuts the door.*)

CATHERINE

I'm sorry, I'm sorry, it won't happen
again; I thought I put it on the latch.

ELIZA

Well, you didn't, and it's winter.
Close it, or we're all going to catch
a real, permanent cold.
And don't let no one enter,
no one, do you hear me, child?
There's people who want him killed.
David Walker, you promised!
Ain't you coming, ain't you gonna dress?
It's Thanksgiving, today is God's business,
not the noise of your printing press.
For the last time. Church. Your promise.

WALKER

I said I wasn't, but yes.
For the last time, though, I promise.
Right, Eliza, I'll come to church,
but I have lost any faith in prayers,
and what I will ask God today is
to deliver me towards evil,
'cause why should all the evil be theirs
and the goodness ours?

(*He picks out a coat from the rack.*)

ELIZA

I won't hear such wickedness.
Not in front of this child.

(*To* CATHERINE)

And you, what you staring at, miss?

CATHERINE

May I say you look very nice?

(*Church bell chimes.*)

ELIZA

Well, that's a piece of good news
for a change. Now, you sew this lapel
    (*She gives* CATHERINE *an old coat to repair.*)
like I showed you, then dice the turkey
for a nice, hot dinner.
David, I can hear the meeting bell
from the Brattle Street chapel.

WALKER

It's tolling for my funeral.

(WALKER *and* ELIZA *walk out into the street. It is snowing.*
Enter CHORUS.)

CHORUS (*Sings.*)

Keep our innocence, Jacob Lawrence;
Horace Pippin, paint our pain.

Romare Bearden, bear our burden,
Deep in the American grain..

WALKER *(Sings.)*

I see a city on a hill,
Its walls as white as snow.
Deliver us from evil:
The red earth and the plough.

CHORUS *(Sings.)*

Romare Bearden, bear our burden,
Horace Pippin, paint our pain.
Keep our innocence, Jacob Lawrence.
Frederick Douglass, lift your pen.

(They walk, in place, towards us, the snow blowing. The
FIGURE *emerges behind them. Fade-out.)*

SCENE THREE

A half hour later. CATHERINE *is setting the small dining*
table, cleaning and singing. Outside, a black man,
BARBADOS, *in a heavy but ragged seafarer's coat, boots, a*

cap approaches the house, a canvas bag slung over his shoulder. He waits, looking at the house, then at a piece of paper, an address. The FIGURE *emerges from the dark.*

CATHERINE (*Sings.*)

Oh, tell them I'll be coming home,
No seas can ever ban me,
Nor pelting gale nor blinding foam,
Until I see Killarney.
I know the sorrow I must bear,
Tears are my rainy parish,
But all I love are waiting there
And speak the Irish language.
For when they take you from your land,
Far, for whatever reason,
Only the heart can understand
Why it commits its treason,
Or why it sanctifies the sound
Of Donegal or Kerry,
Oh, I'll be coming, there I'm bound,
If only in my green memory.

CHORUS (*Sings.*)

Oh, way-la-li, oh, way-la-li,
Oh, way-la-li, way-li-leee,

Oh, I'll be coming, there I'm bound,
If only in my green memory.

BARBADOS

Is this Brattle Street, boss?

FIGURE

Can't you read the sign?

(BARBADOS *goes near the house, peers in through a slit in*
the curtains.)

BARBADOS

And that machine there is the press?

FIGURE

Where're you from, boy?
You a runaway?

BARBADOS

No, sir. I'm—or if you prefer—
I'se free. My name's Barbados. You know that.

FIGURE

Perhaps. Did you jump ship?

BARBADOS

Happy Thanksgiving.

(*He walks towards the house, but turns into the alley. The*
FIGURE *moves off.*)

CATHERINE (*Cleaning and singing.*)
Oh, tell them I'll be coming home,
No seas can ever ban me,
Nor pelting gale nor blinding foam,
Until I see Killarney.
(*She moves towards the rack of used clothes to dust there. The*
clothes part suddenly, BARBADOS *stands among them.*
She screams, steps back.)
Oh God! How did you get in?
I was warned this would happen
if I left the door unlatched.

BARBADOS

I jimmied a back window.
I think he was chopping kindling
and he left his door open.
Mr. Walker is being watched.
(*He goes to the press.*)
Is this machine for ironing?
No. This must be the printing press.
(*He lifts up some type samples.*)

And these are the typesetting letters,
which I can't read. I can't read. Can you?

CATHERINE

I'm learning. He's teaching me.

BARBADOS

And where's he himself, at this hour?

CATHERINE

The Walkers have gone to their chapel.

BARBADOS

The one for soot-skinned Christians.
I've important letters for him.
This pamphlet looks like the Appeal.
Do you know a William Garrison,
a very big man in Boston?
He's Mr. Walker's good friend?
(*He sticks an unlit clay pipe in his mouth.*)

CATHERINE

I have seen him here, I think.
Would you care to sit down?
I have some work to finish
before they come back to dinner.

BARBADOS

So, David Walker's praying? Giving thanks?

CATHERINE

His wife's more the Christian one.

BARBADOS

Them niggers got more faith
than the ones who taught them.
Guess she likes the singing.

CATHERINE

Mrs. Walker took me from the workhouse
to clean and sometimes cook for them.
She's a woman of great charity.
They should be back very soon.

BARBADOS

They got theirselves a white slave.

CATHERINE

They're very charitable people, sir.

BARBADOS

Still, they's niggers like me.

CATHERINE

Maybe that's why, sir.

BARBADOS

Don't "sir" me, miss.
I hate hypocrisy.

CATHERINE

I'm just being polite, sir.

BARBADOS

Know what that coon's plotting to do?

CATHERINE

That what?

BARBADOS

Coon, sambo, jigaboo.
He printed a pamphlet that's being read
from here down to the Carolinas
advocating the uprising of all the other
coons and sambos to kill their masters.
It's outright sedition. He's your master.
Would you kill him, Catherine?
If he reprints that pamphlet,
he's yesterday's gravy. I'm here
to stop him. I brought him letters

from the British abolitionists,
all the way from London to Charleston.
So, you're an orphan, Catherine?

CATHERINE

Aye. My parents perished in the crossing.

BARBADOS

From what, Catherine?

CATHERINE

Pellagra, sir.

BARBADOS

The disease? I know pellagra,
but it sounds like a small town in Italy.
                    (*He sings.*)
Ah, Pellagra, bellissima pellagra.
                    (*Spoken.*)
You've an angel's voice. I heard you singing.
I stood out there on the white street
and heard you singing of how you miss home.
I understand that. And you know why?

CATHERINE

No. Just who might you be, sir, please?

BARBADOS

They call me Barbados, after the island.
You know Cromwell sent a lot of Irish
to Barbados in chains. Just like me.

(*He sings.*)

I been sold in Charleston,
But I broke free,
And when I smell freedom,
It smells of the sea.

CHORUS (*Sings.*)

Away, away,
Away, far away.

BARBADOS (*Sings.*)

In the port of London,
On the shining Thames River,
I heard the bells of chiming iron
Sing, "You're free forever."

CHORUS (*Sings.*)

Sing away,
Away,
Away,
Away.

BARBADOS

Come on, Catherine, sing along.

CATHERINE

I've no voice, sir. Don't have me croakin'.

BARBADOS

You're Irish; it's a reel, a jig.
You can help a poor lost nig
get through with some music and joking.
When I finish the verse, two of us
join in the chorus: (*Sings.*) *Away, away*.

CATHERINE

No, I won't, sir. It's wrong, sir. I won't.

BARBADOS

When did the Almighty ever hate a song?
Come on, help the Irish convicts; sing along.

CATHERINE

Lord help me. Feel like I'm going to die.

BARBADOS (*Sings.*)

Salt beef and pickles for my sin,
Long soaked in brine,

Hardtack biscuits, show me, boatswain,
Where do I sign . . .

CATHERINE (*Sings.*)

Away . . .

BARBADOS

Not yet. Not yet.

(*He sings.*)

Ain't going back to no Charleston.
There's a jail door open wide
And four walls of dripping stone
Without me inside.

(*Spoken.*)

Now.

CHORUS (*Sings.*)

Away, away . . .

BARBADOS *and* CATHERINE (*Sing.*)

Sing away,
Away,
Away,
Away.

(BARBADOS *dances a reel, increasing the tempo.*)

BARBADOS (*Sings.*)

Me in that cold jail lyin'
And the dripping walls so dark;
Let the boatswain keep shanghaiing
More crew, I ain't going back.

In the port of London
The Sunday bells still chime,
But tell the bells I'm gone
Away, I done my time.

(*He yanks* CATHERINE *up to dance. They do the reel.*)

BARBADOS *and* CATHERINE (*Sing.*)

Sing away
Away,
Away,
Away.

(*The dancing stops.*)

BARBADOS (*Sings.*)

I have smelled freedom
And it smells of the sea.
From Charleston to Boston,
There ain't no place for me.

The lights on the Thames River
Shining bright as coins,
But they can keep that silver
For the freedom I smelled once.

Sing away,
Away,
Away,
Away.

(WALKER *and* ELIZA *enter.* ELIZA *screams.* WALKER *rushes*
for the pistol, aims it at BARBADOS.)

WALKER

Turn around! Hands behind your back!

(BARBADOS *doesn't move.*)

ELIZA

Catherine! Who's this? Who let him in?

CATHERINE

Not me. He came in on his own accord.

WALKER

You heard me. Put your hands on your head!

BARBADOS

I'll do either, once you make up your mind.
Either behind my back or on my head.

(*He turns around.*)

ELIZA

And what was all that singing and dancing?
I could hear the commotion out on the street.

(BARBADOS *puts his hands on his head.*)

BARBADOS

We were celebrating my newfound freedom.
You can blame all the jubilation on me.
I'm a courier, Mr. Walker. I got letters
for your good friend Mr. William Garrison
from British abolitionists. I carried them
to avoid search by the Charleston police,
all the way to Boston, to Brattle Street.
They said for certain I would find him here,
and that if by chance I got into trouble,
you could hide me and give me a disguise,
being a dealer in old clothes.

ELIZA

He's a marked man.

BARBADOS

I know. Tell the girl look in my bag,
she'll find the letters.

WALKER

Look in the bag, Catherine.
Who told you to bring the letters to this house?
(CATHERINE *opens the bag, but she is too nervous;* ELIZA
helps her.)
This pistol I got from William Garrison.
I didn't think I'd use it this early
to shoot coons. Sit down at the table.
Catherine's about to serve you your last meal.
(BARBADOS *sits at the table.*)
There's a set of suspenders there on the rack.
Tie his hands, Catherine, and tie them tight.

(CATHERINE *looks in the rack for the suspenders.* WALKER
takes the letters from ELIZA. CATHERINE *ties*
BARBADOS's *wrists.*)

CATHERINE

Please excuse me, Mr. Barbados.

WALKER

Hold the gun on him, Eliza, while I read.

ELIZA

Not me, David Walker.

BARBADOS

One more nigger
trussed like a turkey. Happy Thanksgiving.

WALKER

Eliza, hold the gun. HOLD IT!
(ELIZA *takes the gun, points it at* BARBADOS *with both
hands. They wait as* WALKER *reads the letters.*)
All right, let him loose, Catherine.
Put the gun down, Eliza.

(WALKER *sits down in desolate silence.* CATHERINE *unties*
BARBADOS's *hands.*)

CATHERINE

Please forgive me, Mr. Barbados.

WALKER (*Holding up the letters.*)
These are for Bill Garrison
from the British abolitionists,
advising him that I am threatening their cause
with the rage in my pamphlet. You sure
that these weren't intercepted in Charleston,
then given to you for David Walker?

You say your name's Barbados.
Did they name you for the island?

BARBADOS

I'm a free slave, a sailor
still bound to my fetters.
Was nearly caught in Charleston
for smuggling these sealed letters
from British abolitionists
aboard ship here to Boston.
The sea loosed my ball and chain,
on the sea's the only freedom,
but these could seal my doom,
'cause here I'm breaking the law,
and not only the law, my life
is in the shadow of the gallows,
not the shadow of the cross,
with no children and no wife,
and only my life to lose.

WALKER

I have said my farewell prayers.
I have said my goodbye to God.
Just like William Garrison;
that white boss and I are finished.
Celebration. This deserves a drink.

BARBADOS

You hold it right there, brother.
The devil prophesies this.
I got some barrel-primed Barbados rum.
A toast to our deliverance.
Something in me insists,
despite the ball and chain,
the torture and the whipping,
that all of this's worth the pain;
so all the way up to Boston
from the slave-port of Charleston
they been sealed in my keeping.
Could you hide me overnight?
I got a present of good rum.

WALKER

Sure you can stay overnight,
and, brother, longer. Welcome.
My house is all yours.

(BARBADOS *brings out a bottle of rum.*)

ELIZA

Our house, David. Our house.
Got to get dinner ready, Catherine.
I'll make a pallet for your rest.

BARBADOS

Can't drink hard liquor myself,
I'm just about recovering
from a bout of pellagra
                    (*He winks at* CATHERINE.)
but I'm not averse to a glass
of cider or gooseberry or elderberry wine.

CATHERINE

I'll fetch it, ma'am.

ELIZA

Thank you, Catherine.

BARBADOS

This bottle's better than wine.

WALKER

It's slave-wine, Barbados;
it's made from the sweat and pain
of all our fellow Negroes
cropping cotton, cutting cane.
    (CATHERINE *starts setting the table,* ELIZA *supervising.*
        WALKER *takes* BARBADOS *over to the clothes rack.*)
On your way back, brother,
I can fit you in good secondhand clothes,
will make you look like a free coloured,

because clothes can change your complexion.
So try this on, and the hat, and the gloves,
and even this silver-knobbed cane.

    (*He gives the clothes to* BARBADOS, *who dresses.*)
You inhabit some white man's stale clothes,
wear his rumpled, discarded ideas,
that don't change what we are, Negroes,
who still do what the white man says,
wear his old clothes, do what he does,
but if Catherine's needle could stitch every torn
seam, fix every patch and iron it,
in this snow-white, pietistic town
of Boston, Senator, you'll never run it.
You'll never manage your own government,
in the fabric of your shredded souls,
except you show gratitude for some reach-me-down
garment, like this frock coat, patched with holes.
But this business I seem to be in,
all seams and appearances, brother,
is my outward business; the sign
outside says DAVID WALKER
DEALER IN OLD CLOTHES ON 27 BRATTLE
ST. But inside is another battle
behind the old clothes, the patched seams,
gone put another sign up, WARRIOR
DEALER IN AFRICAN DREAMS.
How you think he looks, Liza?

ELIZA

Oh, I think he looks fine.

BARBADOS (*Strutting.*)

Thank you, thank you, Senators.

WALKER

And what do you think, Catherine?

CATHERINE

A President. A real boyo, sir.

BARBADOS

Hey, brother Walker, this is fun.
I feel like a senator.

WALKER

A selectman, at least.
Not so fast.

BARBADOS

A black congressman, at last!
Ladies and gentlemen, when I get in,
gonna be no more salvation, no more sin,
gonna be no more gamblin', no more cheatin'.
Sorry, Mrs. Walker. I'm sorry, Catherine.

WALKER

That's what they think
about you and me, brother;
this is what they'll always think,
could drive a thinking man to murder
and a sober one to drink.

BARBADOS

Come on, then, Captain. Have a drink.

WALKER (*Reading.*)

*The American Negroes are the only people in the history of
the world, as far as I know, that ever became free without any
effort of their own. They twanged banjos around the railroad
stations . . .*

(BARBADOS *does a slow, parodic shuffle,* WALKER
mimes a banjo.)

. . . sang melodious spirituals [that's you, Liza], *and believed
that some Yankee would soon come along and give each of
them forty acres and a mule.*

BARBADOS

That's what it says? That's written where?

WALKER

Dat's what it done say, heah.

BARBADOS

Can't read no writin', or I'd be fightin'.

WALKER

You too shiftless, coon.

BARBADOS

Forty acres and a mule, for doing nothin'?

WALKER

You struttin' and ruttin' baboon.

BARBADOS

Cut that reading, cut that writing.

WALKER

Keep breedin' and eatin', no fighting, no fighting.

BARBADOS

No more high-falutin' talking.

WALKER (*Sings.*)

My name's Walker, and I'm cake-walking.
I'm happy, I'm feelin' fine.
One of my talents is keeping my balance
On the Mason-Dixon Line. Cool.
Put your coat on, fool.

WALKER *and* BARBADOS (*Dancing and singing.*)
Just a couple of top-hat scarecrows
In snowy cotton fields,
Just a couple of frock-coated Negroes,
Dat's how we feels.

(ELIZA *and* CATHERINE *watch, laughing.*)

WALKER (*Sings.*)
Couple of crows in frock coats
Stuffed with hay,
Protecting the corn and the oats,
Chasing other crows away.

BARBADOS (*Sings.*)
Jest a coupla minstrels
On the Mason-Dixon Line,
Clacking bones for nickels,
Cracking a shoe shine.

WALKER (*Sings.*)
I got a chore for you, boy,
I got a well-paid chore.
Like you to shine my shoe, boy,
Till it looks like a leather mirror.

BARBADOS (*Sings.*)

Looks like a leather mirror
Where I can see my face.
Snap that rag down where you are,
Boy, that's your rightful place.

(CATHERINE *and* ELIZA *applaud.*)

ELIZA

That's enough. Let's sit down to eat.
You here, Mr. Barbados. Catherine.

CATHERINE

Are you sure, Mrs. Walker?

ELIZA

Catherine Healey, sit!

BARBADOS

A toast.
(*He pours a glass of rum, passes it to* WALKER.)

ELIZA

Wait. If this is your last grace, David,
then say it for all of us here.

WALKER

Let Catherine say it. I'll drink this letter.

(*He puts aside the rum. They sit,* DAVID *at the head of the table.* CATHERINE *brings in the turkey.* CATHERINE *sits. They bow their heads as* CATHERINE *begins grace. Outside, the* FIGURE *emerges and patrols the street.*)

ELIZA

Wait, listen. Somebody's singing
out there on Brattle Street.

(*They wait. Silence.*)

WALKER

Liza, it's just your own ears ringing
from that hymn singing. Let's eat.

(*They settle,* ELIZA *and* CATHERINE *serve.*)

FIGURE (*Sings.*)

Passing the orange windows
Of this bleak November night
With fine families glowing indoors
In the pumpkin-coloured light
Of Thanksgiving's rituals,

Through an early snow that falls white
As the napkins shaken over tables
The streetlamps flickering like candles
With custom and with rite,

(*All bow their heads.* ELIZA *says grace.*)

ELIZA

Mighty God, look after us all
and deliver us from evil, amen.

FIGURE (*Sings.*)

The wanderer and the pilgrim
See corn crucified on the door
And the grace of faces that fills them
With the snow's silent choir
For the steaming victuals,
The dressing and the dewy bowls
In the rites of the feast that falls
In blessing that enshrines their souls
Like light through a forest.

CATHERINE

Holy Mary, Mother of God, pray for us sinners now and
at the hour of our death, amen.

FIGURE (*Sings.*)

May faith reinforce our duty.

May prayer strengthen our resolve

To preserve such simple beauty

In the hunger for His love,

Against evil that belittles

Such sanctities and customs

That show through the frosting glass

Till the perfect kingdom comes

With grace that will never pass.

ELIZA

David, it's your turn. Head of the table.

David Walker, your turn to say grace.

FIGURE (*Sings.*)

The laughing wheat-headed children,

Their apple-glowing parents

In rites devout and Christian

As their napkins' innocence,

Whatever it entails.

Protect them from dark that surrounds

Them, along this candlelit street

As the watchman makes his rounds,

Snow crunched under his feet.

(*They wait.*)

WALKER

All right, then. Grace.

FIGURE

Eat, and be thankful, boy. Eat.

(GARRISON *approaches the* FIGURE *with a package.*)

GARRISON

You've swayed for hours on this street,
dying from hunger. I brought you some meat.
Respect my charity, as I respect your hate.
They are eating. You, too, should eat.

FIGURE

I took a vow. Later. Later I'll eat.
                  (*He puts the meat into his coat.*)
Your warm heart is somethin'
I really do admire.
It's too cold for this business.
I've a powerful feelin' to go in
and warm my hands by the fire.

GARRISON

If the plague is deep in us,
and our vows are thieves,
then he is like Oedipus,

and Boston is Thebes.
If from his horror, blindness
has seared his own eyes,
then isn't our human kindness
the best of remedies?
There are such embittered lines
now, around his mouth,
a mask made from his wanderings
and memories of the South,
but even here in the North,
in this beacon, the city,
the plague spreads, and its truth
is past all our pity.
Its shame is diurnal,
it corrupts the Sabbath,
and the path of Freedom's Journal
is to him the wrong path,
the tame path; the wrong path,
from where his heart was housed.
The wrath of David is the wrath
of Africa aroused;
aroused by exasperation
in this beacon, this city,
by the deceit of patience,
by hypocritical pity.

FIGURE

You can call it hypocritical
all you like, but to me,
this isn't my city, first of all,
and last and first, it's political
and practical, necessity.
Sure, slavery is pitiful,
nobody can turn his back
on that truth, but what's here is full
of murderous venom, an attack
on the white populations, citizens
of the same idea that frees him,
but this Article urges violence,
massacre, and revenge;
it makes all of us victims,
so it's plain self-defence
unless the victim pities him,
pities the murderer
who slashes his throat.
David Walker will go no further
with this published threat.

GARRISON

Pity is easy. What is harder is love.
What is it we're so afraid of?

FIGURE

This black tide, like oil

creeping over our soil

until we are white gulls that beat

in the slick and the black slime

of harbours, in the rack of the sunset,

from Maine to Narragansett.

I see this coming in time,

for all of this man's labours

are not for his people's freedom

but for our final defeat.

The two cannot be separated,

and I have this vision of the tide

of an Africa, suppressed and hated,

creeping over the map of these States,

the inevitable shadow of night.

GARRISON

Sir, is it inevitable?

(*Tribal drumming and chanting, growing louder.*)

FIGURE (*Louder.*)

Open the floodgates wide, sirs,

and if you aren't careful,

a Niagara of niggers,

a black waterfall

sounding like tribal drums,
will drown, drown us all,
and with this white pamphlet comes
a roaring in our ears,
a civic, a national turmoil
of massacre, revolution:
And what is its solution?
No, not your freedom at all,
but murder, and slyly, all at once
a trickle, a cautious sluice
will start pouring till it grows,
till your streets are full of Negroes
raping, burning, screaming;
that's what you must see as real,
not your abolitionist's zeal
in your rag, *The Freedom News,*
this black Niagara
that drowns you in its noise.

(*Tribal chorus, drums.*)

CHORUS (*Warriors in Yoruba.*)
Olutorin
Omo okunkun lorin
Tannatanna tonfo ninu imole atupa re
Tokunlo tokunbo
Bonrin labele, tonrin labemi

Iwin tonrin larin iwin
Tonrobo ko ko ko lati igbale osugbo

ELIZA (*Sings.*)
I see the snow whitening, whitening
Your body, your language, our life.
I was crouching over somebody
In the snow of an alley,
The flakes powdering my face.
I was crouching over your body.
I peeled back the snow's white sheet
And there you was.

WALKER
Were, were.

ELIZA (*Sings.*)
There you was, David Walker,
Stove-grey marble from head to feet.

WALKER
What language you singin' in, Liza?

ELIZA
My language, David. Mine!

(BARBADOS *rises as if in a trance, swaying at the table.*)

ELIZA *and* CHORUS

Olutonrin

Omo okunkun lorin

To npaturpa ile se imole

To nrin ninu ogbo tannatanna

Nigbati erin ba wo

Nigbati erin ba wo

GARRISON

I understand what you mean.

He was one of the noblest of men,

but I understand what you mean.

(*Drumming and chanting.*)

SCENE FOUR

ELIZA *lighting lamps,* CATHERINE *washing up,* WALKER
and BARBADOS *playing cards, the bottle of rum
between them.*

ELIZA (*Sings.*)

This is my fortress,
These lamps in the darkness
Against the surrounding night;
This is my fear, bolting each door, this
Siege, that no enemy can enter
'Cause it's winter
And the night is white.

CHORUS (*Sings.*)

Sobbin' women,
No more sobbin' women.

ELIZA (*Sings.*)

This is my dark prayer
For the dark child within me,
Knowing that it will not be so.
I have seen a shadow cross the window,
Come from the conspiring snow,
That a rose-warm day could be coming when
Sunrise shows through the glass,
Another world for us women
And our children.
I pray it may come to pass.

CHORUS (*Sings.*)

Romare Bearden, bear our burden,
Horace Pippin, paint our pain.
Keep our innocence, Jacob Lawrence,
Frederick Douglass, lift your pen.

ELIZA

Come on, Catherine. Take that basket.
Help me to carry things. Say goodbye.
And take these old clothes with us
to give charity to the Mission.

(CATHERINE *collects a basket and some old clothes.*)

CATHERINE

Goodbye, sir. Mr. Barbados.

BARBADOS

Bye-bye, young lady. Keep your eyes bright.
You're a pure, fine-finished soul.

(CATHERINE *goes up to* WALKER.)

CATHERINE

Sir, I'll see you tomorrow. Goodbye.

WALKER

There are souls who drift like angels

through our turmoil, Catherine Healey,

and if there are visible angels

to be seen, I'll see you tomorrow.

CATHERINE

Are you printing the pamphlet, sir?

WALKER

You know I must do it, Catherine.

Go. An innocence like yours

could deter me from my task.

(CATHERINE *exits*. ELIZA *goes up to* BARBADOS.)

ELIZA

Will you excuse us a little?

BARBADOS

                Oh, me? Oh, most assuredly.

I could fetch in some more kindling.

And I could get me a coal shovel

I seen propped up by the door

to scrape up some piling snow.

A man's got to earn his supper.

WALKER

(He puts on his sailor's coat and cloth cap, exits. In a while,
we hear him singing his chantey and scraping snow in
the yard.)

ELIZA

I don't trust him, David.
He ain't one of us.
I don't trust his eyes.

WALKER

Liza, that's the look we get
when you're somebody who hid
from something; you can never forget
the pain of their injustice.

ELIZA

Then all of us, all of us
should have those eyes. Careful,
don't do nothing you'll regret.

WALKER

All day you been fearful,
nagging me to death:
Be careful, David, be careful.
That ain't no way to greet
a brother, one of our brothers.

Barbados is my brother,
now you just quit picking on me.

ELIZA

Judas was Jesus' brother,
he had the same look in his eyes,
and Jesus saw it; now here's another
Judas sitting inside my own house.
Well, you ain't paying that price.
I just don't trust him, please.
I don't trust his restless eyes.
He's the wrong kind of Negro,
and you should know what I mean.

WALKER

      Well, if so,

he has a right to be evil
as much as any white man,
to vote for the party of the devil
as opposed to the Christian.
Why are all these figures rearin'
from the mist and marshes of your mind,
all that Carolina kind of conjurin'
making beads of sweat on your brow?
All that cotton-country wisdom? Listen,
you got to learn to leave such behind.

WALKER

(CATHERINE *comes back in.*)

CATHERINE

Are you coming, Missus Walker?

(*She waits.*)

ELIZA

I don't want to leave you, David.

WALKER

Go on now, what's the matter? Go on.

ELIZA

I just don't want to leave you with him.

WALKER

You ain't starting all that again?

ELIZA

But I made this promise to the Women's Union.

WALKER

And they expecting the cakes and the wine.

ELIZA

It's the annual sale and bazaar.

WALKER

You told me before, I'll be fine.

ELIZA

It's the Anti-Slavery Bazaar. White women.

WALKER

It's a good cause. And you take Catherine.

(*He leads them to the door, and they exit. He comes back towards the press.* BARBADOS *enters.*)

BARBADOS

Where's the rum, sir?

WALKER

Brother.

BARBADOS

Brother. My hands are numb.
(*He salutes* WALKER.)
Sir, your servant: Corporal Barbados!
What are our orders for tomorrow?

(WALKER *goes to the window, parts the curtain, shouts at the street.*)

WALKER

To answer excess with excess,

that is, to return a horror

even worse than its origin,

that will make its creators exclaim:

Brutal, coarse, uncivilized,

wild beasts who leap over the boundaries

of our polite persecution.

(He returns to the press.)

Tonight I will go to press,

pamphlets will pour from that bed,

and tomorrow thousands of them

will be swiftly circulated

by hand all over this city,

and not in this city alone.

Then, when our madness is marshaled

into a tattered army, when the cry

goes up in the streets to slaughter,

then to watch our enemies die

will be as simple, as the pamphlet says,

as drinking a glass of water.

Torches and muskets, Africa

like a lion out on those streets.

(The FIGURE *reappears. Drumming, shouting,*
sounds of revolt.)

But the Garrisons want a discreet

liberation, emancipating that's neat.

Only Boston is allowed to revolt
the way it was decently done.
Our liberal deliverers want
a decent black revolution.
(*The* FIGURE *flaps his arms from the cold, paces faster. The
drums and shouting fade.*)
A toast! To our victory!
(WALKER *pours from the rum bottle, offers a drink to*
BARBADOS, *who shakes his head, refusing; then* BARBADOS
takes the rum bottle slowly from WALKER, *who staggers and
pitches to the floor.*)
You betrayed me. Didn't you?

BARBADOS

Yes.

WALKER

Take me to a doctor. I beg you.

BARBADOS

No.

WALKER

What brought you to such wickedness?

BARBADOS

You, man. You.

WALKER

Me. Why do you say that? In my own house?

BARBADOS

Why do I say that? 'Cause it's business.

WALKER

Business?

BARBADOS

Correct. You bought my freedom.
Freedom is my reward, yes.

WALKER

I'm glad I was of some service.
(He tries to rise.)

BARBADOS

So am I.

WALKER

Get me to a doctor, or get one for me.

BARBADOS

You don't get it, brother?
I'm free when you die.

WALKER

You'll be just as free if I live.

BARBADOS

You ain't got half the money they can give.
Stay in here, by the fire, it's warm in here.
It's cold out in the world, David, brother.
You know it's cold out there.
Now I got to go meet this representative.

(*He covers* WALKER *in old clothes, exits into the snow.
Outside . . .*)

BARBADOS

Where you, man? Said where you at, man?

(*The* FIGURE *emerges.*)

FIGURE

Is it done?

BARBADOS

In a lil' while.

FIGURE

We're pleased it went according to plan.

BARBADOS

Don't start talkin' nothin' 'bout the divine will.
I done a great, great wrong.

FIGURE

You'll soon be free of this evil.
To whom do you belong?

BARBADOS

Neither you nor the devil,
I belong to me.
So, no more ball and chain.
Nor the sea's wild commotion.
Nor the lighthouses of stars
on the sky's black ocean.
Ten thousand, and freedom.

FIGURE

You got the figure wrong.
If only you could read
the small print or the large
on the white snow of this pamphlet,
you'd be free of that mirage.
One thousand for him dead.
Ten thousand for him alive.

(*He shows* BARBADOS *the reward poster, then puts it away.*)

BARBADOS

That's not what you people said.

FIGURE

That's not what I said, boy,
or what you still can't read.
Your ship's still on the bay, boy,
anchored in the homestead.
There's print and there's talk.
Can you read your contract?

BARBADOS

No, I can't read. Not like him.

FIGURE

'Cause that's what you signed.

BARBADOS

I can't read no letterin'.
I might as well of been blind.

FIGURE

So you can't read this contract?

BARBADOS

Be Christ, I said no.

FIGURE

These black marks like your footprints
on the page of the snow?
Then you should read before you act.

BARBADOS

Look, I want my money now.
I want my freedom now.
And that's all I know.

(WALKER *rises, comes through the door, out into the
snowy street.*)

FIGURE

There's print and there's talkin'.
Who the devil is that there?

BARBADOS

Jesus Christ! He's dead.

FIGURE

Then that's a dead man walkin'.

BARBADOS

I can't finish him off.
If he's livin', pay me.
Anything would be enough.

He's only walkin' towards his grave.
In a minute he'll be dead.
Trust me and trust the poison.
Watch him. He'll be dead soon.
Look, I'll take what you have.

FIGURE

That's what I'm afraid of. You want him dead,
or you want him livin',
dead is a thousand dollars
and that's all I'm givin'.

BARBADOS

Give me the ten thousand,
can't you see he's still alive?

FIGURE

The payment is in my hand,
and that's all I can give, brother.
That is all I am giving.
He is neither one nor the other,
so here is your reward;
the job you did is over,
you failed to keep your word.

(*He shoots* BARBADOS. WALKER *staggers on in the snow.*)

BARBADOS

Stop, stop walking, help me,
get me to a doctor.
Help me, help me,
or I'll die soon.

(*The* FIGURE *fires at* WALKER.)

FIGURE

Stop, you black fiend of infamy,
stop. Lie down, die, stop walking.

BARBADOS

Help me, help me. This is my own poison.
Watch out for the Figure.

(*He dies.*)

WALKER

Who sent you? Who sent you?
All day I have seen your figure.

FIGURE

The moon is a white eye, nigger,
so just say the man in the moon.

(WALKER *collapses. The* FIGURE *removes a piece of bread*
from his coat, eats, then moves off, away from the body.

ELIZA *enters the street. Snow. Then* CATHERINE. ELIZA
stands over WALKER's *body.*)

ELIZA (*Sings.*)

I wasn't wrong.
Goliath won,
Goliath won.
David is slain,
David is slain,
Goliath won again.
O child in my belly,
O my Absalom,
See your father where he lie
In the snows of Boston?
Forgive their pity,
Rise up, David, walk home
To that other kingdom
'Cause you gon' be forgotten
Like a blot,
Like a spot
On the white shirt of this city.

(GARRISON *enters. The* FIGURE *can be seen in the distance.*
GARRISON *sees it, then turns away.*)

GARRISON (*Sings.*)

I could weep like David, Liza,

Over Absalom, his son,

But David is now Absalom.

I see him lying there

Like the branch that kept the ransom

Of his beautiful hair.

It's clear in your tears, Liza,

Your mirrored accusation

Over the thing that lies there,

But I was not the one.

I loved him like my own son.

ELIZA (*Sings.*)

Smooth the brown wrinkled Mississippi of his brow.

Before the fresh drifts get dirty

Under their indifferent shoes

On Beacon Street, or Brattle,

On any street you choose.

Let warriors lift him, for his battle

Is over, and cut on his stone

David Walker, 1785–1830.

Soft snow's falling on Boston

Like Carolina cotton,

On Nigger Hill, on Faneuil Hall,

On the street known as Beacon.

No more sobbin', no more speakin',

Only silence, that be all.
Take him softly, David Walker,
Through the white snowfall.
　(She falls, rises, then walks steadily behind the WARRIOR
　cortege. Slow drums, tribal wail. The singer playing ELIZA
　removes bits of her costume, makeup, wig, stands bare in
　　　　　　　　　ordinary light.)
I played a woman named Eliza Walker.
David Walker her husband,
in the city we see outside
us, and the one we can't see inside,
whatever the city is named;
a husband in whom I took pride,
and some of you will be ashamed
of this violence for which he died,
and some will be satisfied.
　　　　　　　(She exits.)

　　　CHORUS *(Sings.)*
Romare Bearden, bear our burden,
Horace Pippin, paint our pain.
Jacob Lawrence, paint our innocence,
Dyed in the American grain.

END

THE GHOST DANCE

·

For Duncan Smith and
Robert Bensen

The Ghost Dance was commissioned by Hartwick College, Oneonta, and was produced there in November 1989. It was directed by Duncan Smith and designed by Richard and Sally Montgomery. The principal cast was as follows:

CATHERINE WELDON —*Elizabeth Kuempel*
KICKING BEAR —*Shane Barbanel*
MAJOR JAMES MCLAUGHLIN —*Hugh Timoney*
DR. JEREMY BEDDOES —*Duncan Smith*

CAST OF CHARACTERS
(IN ORDER OF APPEARANCE)

CATHERINE WELDON, *a widow*

KICKING BEAR, *a Sioux Indian*

SERGEANT MICHAEL PATRICK DONNELLY

CORPORAL QUINT, *the paymaster*

TROOPERS

INDIAN, *at the General Store*

MAJOR JAMES MCLAUGHLIN, *Indian agent*

LIEUTENANT BRANDON, *Lucy's fiancé*

DR. JEREMY BEDDOES, *Army surgeon*

JAMES EAGLE, *Indian lay preacher*

LUCY, *or* SWIFT RUNNING DEER, *Eagle's daughter*

SECRETARY FOR INDIAN AFFAIRS

GENERAL, *at the fort*

CHURCH CONGREGATION, *also* INDIAN GHOST
    DANCERS

SARAH QUINN, *pioneer woman*

FIDDLERS

OFFICERS

LADIES

DRUNKS

SENTRY

MRS. MCLAUGHLIN

PLACE: *North Dakota, 1890*

TIME: *late fall*

NOTE ON THE STAGING

There are several changes of locale. These changes and, indeed, more important than the changes, the play should be performed fluently and simply, like Indian theatre, with minimal props, with blankets, poles, and flags to indicate locations, and with minimal furniture.

ACT ONE

SCENE ONE

Stage right: The parlour and kitchen of the Parkin Ranch. A rug. A low table with pots. Late afternoon. CATHERINE *is baking. She pours flour into a pan.*
Stage left: A small stand of birches. An Indian, KICKING BEAR, *is in the birches, light snow powdering his blanket, his hair, his face white. He holds a lance.* CATHERINE *dusts her palms, goes to the door. She looks for a good while at the Indian, then returns to her baking. Lights fade.*

SCENE TWO

The same, but by lamplight. CATHERINE *is wearing a robe, her hair loosened. She carries a lamp to the door.* KICKING BEAR *is in the moonlit birches, nearer.* CATHERINE *watches him for a while, then, lowering the wick of the lamp, enters her bedroom. She pauses, picks up a child's hobby horse made of a carved horse's head on a stick, then puts it in a corner. Lights fade.*

SCENE THREE

The same. Next morning. KICKING BEAR *has crossed into the parlour. He squats on the rug. A rolled-up package is next to him with the lance.* CATHERINE, *dressed, squats near her pots, baking.*

CATHERINE

I should go back to Boston, to streetlights and carriages,
long white gloves and concerts, and velvet waiters
drawing back your chair, to find another husband.
But I'm stuck out here on the farm, alone.
The Parkins have decided to sell the place,
and they're back East. I'm tempted myself,
in these iron winters of North Dakota.
I've been chattering to myself for two months now,
so you don't have to talk. I'm used to silence.

KICKING BEAR

Whisky.

CATHERINE

Well, you took the word right out of my mouth!
  (*She exits, returns with a bottle of whisky and two glasses.*
  She puts the whisky out of his reach, then brings a platter
  of doughnuts.)
But before whisky, eat.

KICKING BEAR

Whisky.

CATHERINE

No whisky. Eat.
You stood out there two days and nights.

What made you come in?

(KICKING BEAR *reaches for the whisky, but* CATHERINE

moves it, pushing the platter of doughnuts towards him.)

Maybe you and me'll get howling drunk

after you eat. But they're damn good doughnuts.

Careful now, they're hot.

(KICKING BEAR *puts a finger through a doughnut,*

shows CATHERINE.)

KICKING BEAR

Wagon wheel.

(*He spins it on his finger.*)

No food. Whisky.

CATHERINE

No. Oh, goddamn it, it's your funeral.

(*She pours him a shot, which he gulps, then another; then she*

pours herself one and moves the platter nearer.)

Hi, Kicking Bear. Hi, hi, do you remember me?

Mrs. Catherine Weldon, of course you remember me.

I had the distinction, in Colonel Cody's circus,

of being Sitting Bull's secretary. So tell me,

what message did he send me, the old bullfrog?

KICKING BEAR (*Pointing to whisky.*)

More.

CATHERINE

No. No more whisky. Eat.

(*She moves the whisky, then the platter.* KICKING BEAR
unfolds his package—a portrait of Sitting Bull. He indicates:
"You painted that" to CATHERINE, *who nods.*)

Yes, I painted it. It's a true likeness.

(KICKING BEAR *unwraps the contents of the package—*
some china cups and saucers.)

A door-to-door salesman. Not today, thank you.

Not today, thank you. Not today, try next door.

Not today, because I sent him these presents.

When presents are returned, friendship is dead.

This is what he sent you so far to tell me?

(KICKING BEAR *is silent.*)

So now he's trying to make me his enemy?

I rode out to see him on the Reservation

on a sparkling morning in late September,

with the leaves turning, wondering if he'd changed

from the friend I had made in Colonel Cody's circus,

and I felt eyes stalking me through the wild corn

that was rustling its bonnets, and my horse sensed it,

when a fence of warriors sprung up in the road.

They were as thin as rakes, their faces painted white,

and I nearly tumbled. But one held my horse

and pulled us around, then another one commanded

that I return to the farm. I said I was worried

about the menacing thunderhead growing between

the Sioux and the Army. Still they refused,

so I gave him these presents here to remind him.

Were those the Ghost Dancers, who wouldn't let me

through?

(*Silence.*)

KICKING BEAR

Listen!

(*He grabs her arm.*)

Listen! Stop pitying yourself.

This thing happened to him on his own land.

One day he was out looking for his old circus horse

when a lark sang to him from the ladder of the sun:

"Your own people will kill you." So the lark sang.

He is very afraid of the Indian Agency,

of Major McLaughlin and his Indian police.

The Ghost Dancers will gather at Standing Rock,

at the edge of that place where they chased the buffalo,

to leap to their death and be smashed like this.

(*He smashes a cup, then a saucer.*)

Now you understand.

CATHERINE

No, I don't. I refuse to understand.

I understand I have made an oath of friendship

which doesn't break like crockery. Tell him that.

I understand that I've made these doughnuts
the way I used to prepare my boy's breakfast
and I don't like them wasted. Do you understand?
No. You refuse to. You're one of them, aren't you?
                    (*Silence. She laughs.*)
I ordered these from Boston, they're part of a set.
                    (*She collects the pieces.*)
But my friendship won't get cold like some doughnut.
What is the Ghost Dance? A madness that began
with a crazy Paiute prophet in western Nevada
and it's caught on like the cholera, or whisky,
till you all believe it will bring resurrection,
but before you're resurrected you have to get cold.
And I am telling you now, your prophet is mad.
He preached that an Indian Messiah, like ours,
will ride from the West with the dead Indian warriors
returning to their earth, with the sunrise behind them,
with buffalo and horses, and that your Messiah
will make the Army vanish with his magic,
as long as you people dance the Ghost Dance,
and maybe it's possession no different from
all our singing and clapping. But Sitting Bull,
I know Sitting Bull is too smart to believe it.
If he's assembling the dancers to fight a last battle,
the Army will make him a ghost faster than he thinks.
Now we're through talking. For God's sake, eat.

(KICKING BEAR *rises, paces the house.*)

KICKING BEAR

How can I eat? You know our starvation.

You know that McLaughlin cut down on our rations.

It is autumn now. As it is with those leaves,

so it will be with all the Indian nations.

You will hear the silent noise of their wailing

in the freezing wind, their branches begging.

And food will fall like flour, but who can eat the snow?

The fire will die in the heart, and white smoke

will blow across Makoce Sica, Land-That-Gives-Back-
  Nothing.

The herds of buffalo will blow like black smoke.

The buffalo already are becoming ghosts;

they will run across the plains with soft thunder,

when all the red tribes are blown across the earth,

the Blackfoot, the Sioux, the Ogalalas, the Cheyennes,

and their leaves will be buried in your whiteness,

a whiteness with no memory, like the deep snow.

They will fade like weevils in a bag of flour

denied us by the agency. They want us to fade,

but let me tell you, Lady from the East,

if you say you love us, then suffer with us,

when the snow spins, and the white wind screams

through the skeletons of birches, with the Ghost Dance,

let our screams come from the cave of your mouth,

let wild ice grip the roots of your hair,
share in a famine to join all the ghosts
of the Blackfoot, the Sioux, the Ogalalas, the Cheyennes,
because Sitting Bull will not see you anymore.

CATHERINE

I'll not lose my friendship to please his enemies.
Some white faces can keep their vows, you know.
I will find out whatever I can to help him.

(*Silence. A horse whinnies in the distance.*)

KICKING BEAR

That is my horse in the pines. He must be hungry.
I'll bring him these.
(*He picks up the doughnuts.*)
I will change his name.
From now on he'll be the Horse That Eats Doughnuts.
(*He goes to the door, pauses.*)
You have a son. Where is he? A fine boy.

CATHERINE

I left him down the Cannonball River
with a friend of mine. He had an accident.
A rusty nail pricked him and the foot infected.
I smothered his fever like a fire, with blankets,
and took him downriver.

KICKING BEAR

And not to the fort?
The Army has a doctor in the fort. Beddoes.

CATHERINE

I've heard about the Army doctor at the fort,
that he drinks too much and talks even more,
that he believes in nothing, and hates your people,
so I took my chance on the Cannonball instead.
I used Indian medicine and the cool river helped him
and the care of the great woman, the widow Quinn,
since I promised I'd look after the Parkin ranch.
Two warriors took us down in a big canoe.

KICKING BEAR

To put your faith in the Cannonball River
and use our medicine, instead of the Army,
that is very Indian.

CATHERINE

Well, perhaps I'm Indian. Okay?
At any rate, I don't see any difference.
I don't think it is a question of changing faith.

KICKING BEAR (*In Sioux, with a sign.*)
Goodbye.

CATHERINE

Not goodbye, Kicking Bear.

Anyway, goodbye is just another beginning.

Tell him I will find out the plans from the fort.

(KICKING BEAR *exits.* CATHERINE *rolls up the mat, the portrait, and exits as* KICKING BEAR *climbs through the birches to the far sound of a bugle.*)

SCENE FOUR

Parade ground. The fort. Young TROOPERS *with lances, carrying pennons, are lined up, but at ease.* SERGEANT DONNELLY, *in red undershirt, suspenders, loosened jacket, cap, cigar stub, boots, striped trousers, is inspecting the patrol; behind him* CORPORAL QUINT, *the paymaster, carries a notebook.* SERGEANT DONNELLY *is carrying an Indian shirt behind his back. He paces, wheels, stops. His voice is hoarse from bad whisky.*

DONNELLY (*Shouts.*)

TROOPERS!

(*He clears his throat.*)

Jaysus! Who said that? The whisky. The ghost of pure moonshine, Mr. Quint.

(*He tries again, thumps his chest.*)

TROOPERS! The flower and pride of the U.S. Army, lads that I love like me own sons. You're looking at a veteran of the Little Big Horn.

(*He whips out the painted shirt.*)

Yer looking at a chance to be invisible! I've worn it meself and survived many a battle. Because this here's some captured shirt worn by our haythen enemy, which bullets whistle through, conferrin' the glory of the invisibility on youse, and I, Sergeant Michael Patrick Donnelly, am the living testimony that it works, because yer can't see me now, can yer? So, were I to put this shirt on in the height of the battle 'twould be a case of disappearin' Donnelly. And a case of—

(*He looks around in mock panic.*)

—"Where is the man? He was here recently." So I've got some on order that were captured from the enemy. And Paymaster Quint there is here to take down your sizes and to accept an advance of a dollar from each of you, as of now! Take their order, Paymaster. If ye've no money now, 'twill be docked from your pay by Mr. Quint himself. But you lads will be thankful that Michael Patrick Donnelly conferred immortality on you when you next engage the heathen with his own magic charms. Trooper Williams, me daisy, can Mr. Quint put you down for a painted shirt, then? One painted shirt. Trooper Williams, a bargain.

WILLIAMS

Yes, sir, Sergeant.

QUINT

What size collar, Trooper Williams? Collar and elbow.

WILLIAMS

I'd say fifteen and a half, Corporal Quint. I'm not sure.

DONNELLY

Measure the man for a shirt or a coffin! Why do they send us these boys? Measure him, measure him, Mr. Quint, collar to elbow. Hold his lance for him, Trooper. Better to be measured for a shirt than a coffin, correct, Trooper Williams?

(QUINT *begins measuring* TROOPER WILLIAMS.)

SCENE FIVE

Same time. On the opposite side of the stage, an INDIAN *sets
up a trestle with blankets, pots, in the General Store. The*
INDIAN *is in Western clothes, hat, waistcoat.* CATHERINE
enters, shopping. She inspects a blanket. MAJOR
MCLAUGHLIN *enters the store, stands close to* CATHERINE.
DONNELLY *and* QUINT *are on the parade ground.*

MCLAUGHLIN

Careful he doesn't sell you some stale blanket
he's washed over, with the cholera still in it.
Besides, we have enough at the agency
to spare you a couple. It would cost you nothing.
James McLaughlin.

CATHERINE

I know. No thanks.
I'd rather buy them. You're not permitted
to give away government issue, Major.

MCLAUGHLIN

They're going to court-martial me for two blankets?
You stay here and I'll fetch them from the post.
I'll just have them issued by the quartermaster.

CATHERINE

Please. Excuse me. But I want nothing from the Army.
Oh, very well. Once you don't get into trouble.

MCLAUGHLIN

The Army owes me more than two scraggy blankets.
And I owe you more than the Army.

CATHERINE

What does that mean?

MCLAUGHLIN

I've stood outside my office every Wednesday,
once I realized that your shopping for supplies
had the same pattern, and watched you ride by
the Indian Agency in your trap. It's a sight
I've looked forward to for the last two months,
so I owe you that pleasure more than I owe the government
or the Army anything.

CATHERINE

You waited for my trap?

MCLAUGHLIN

That's correct, Mrs. Weldon. The one with the pony.
Every Wednesday at ten.

CATHERINE

What about the other trap?
Affection? Maybe I've enjoyed your watching me.

MCLAUGHLIN

Well, if that's your idea of what a trap is, ma'am,
then that's a sweet prison to look forward to.
As well as the blankets. I'll go fetch them now.

(*He tips his hat, exits. He crosses the dusty street. Two*
TROOPERS *pass.* CATHERINE *leans against the counter*
trestle, watching him. The INDIAN *packs up the blankets. She*
does not turn; her eyes are on MCLAUGHLIN.)

(*Stage right: The parade ground.* LIEUTENANT BRANDON
enters, surveys the scene, walks up to DONNELLY.)

BRANDON

What, in God's name, are you doin', Donnelly?

DONNELLY

Keep measurin'.

(*The* TROOPERS *stamp to attention.*)

BRANDON

At ease. Stop measuring. STOP MEASURING!
(*The* TROOPERS *stand at ease.*)
What are these shirts?
Whose are these shirts?

(*He takes the shirts from* QUINT.)

DONNELLY

What shirts? Oh, I didn't see them, sir. They're
often guilty of invisibility. If it's these shirts
you mean, sir, I was simply taking orders.

BRANDON

Well, you can take my order, both of you. STOP IT!

(DONNELLY *inspects the* TROOPERS, *adjusting their*
uniforms, as QUINT *takes measurements.*)

DONNELLY

For indeed, not in word, but in deed, we've fought
them all, haven't we, Paymaster Quint?

QUINT

Aye, Patrick. Side by side. Lift your elbow, Trooper.

DONNELLY

Aye! Fought those naked, dog-eatin' haythen, the Messy
Breeches, the Look-Alike-As, the Sew-Your-Patches, and
paid dearly for it, too, didn't I, Mr. Quint? On me own cross
(*He rolls up his shirt and shows an ugly scar across
his stomach.*)
like this from the lance of a Sioux at Little Big Horn.
We didn't marry them either. We fought them.
Not fondle their squaws, smellin' of buffalo grease.

BRANDON

And, for that remark, Donnelly, you're fightin' me.
(*He removes his jacket.*)
It's a personal insult to my fiancée, and I'm handling
it personally. People like you are a disgrace to the
Army. And I'm not going to hide behind my ranking.

DONNELLY (*Removing his jacket.*)

Would you take care of this for me, Paymaster Quint,
while I have a discussion with this pretty officer?

(*He hands* QUINT *the jacket.* DONNELLY *and* BRANDON
begin to fight. The TROOPERS *form a circle.* BRANDON *can
box.* DONNELLY *is a swinger, barroom style.* BRANDON *falls
down, rises, falls down again, rises.* MCLAUGHLIN *arrives,
the* TROOPERS *stand back. Across the street, at the entrance
of the General Store,* CATHERINE *is watching.*)

MCLAUGHLIN

That's enough, that's enough now, gentlemen. Goddamn you, Donnelly, I said, Enough!

(*He pushes* DONNELLY *away from* BRANDON, *whose mouth is bleeding.* DONNELLY *kicks at* MCLAUGHLIN, *who catches his heel and spins him around.* DONNELLY *falls. The* TROOPERS *cheer.* BRANDON *puts on his jacket.*)

DONNELLY

The Secretary of the Bureau, lads, is coming to find out if the esteemed Mr. McLaughlin here's losin' control of his Indians. And whether he's exceedin' his position since he's not in the regular Army but simply a civilian major. I suggest the Indian agent look after Indian Affairs, and not interfere in the business of the Army. I suggest . . .

(*He swings again at* MCLAUGHLIN, *who steps back and draws a pistol from his holster.*)

MCLAUGHLIN

I suggest you sober up, Sergeant Donnelly, and not worry about my ranking, and the same for you, Lieutenant Brandon.

BRANDON

I don't take orders from you, McLaughlin, I can handle this.

DONNELLY

They're both with squaw women, you understand, lads. They both married the enemy. And this one with the pistol got his rankin' from the circus. Colonel Wild Bill Cody's Wild West Circus, I believe. You draw a pistol on me again, Major, and you'd better worry how you sleep nights.

(*He exits, trailing his jacket.*)

BRANDON

Troopers, dismissed.
Stay out of the Army's fights, Mr. McLaughlin.
I said DISMISSED.

(*The* TROOPERS *march off. Exit* BRANDON. QUINT *picks up the shirts, is about to leave.*)

MCLAUGHLIN

Corporal Quint, I want you to follow me to the quarter-master's stores and carry two blankets from the Indian Agency to that lady standing there near her trap. You will do as I tell you, Quint. Follow me.

(*He salutes* CATHERINE, *exits with* QUINT. *Lights fade.*)

SCENE SIX

The Army doctor's office. DR. BEDDOES. MCLAUGHLIN *is putting on his shirt. A trestle with a basin, rags.*

MCLAUGHLIN

I don't know why I'm here, Doctor. I daresay I am
exhausted by all the brutality, I suppose. The rib's not
broken?
Why the hell should I fight a fool like Donnelly?

DR. BEDDOES

There's nothing wrong with you, Jim. It'll pass.

MCLAUGHLIN

Major was my title in Buffalo Bill's circus.
Why do we pale faces presume our superiority?
Good God, Jeremy, I married an Indian.

DR. BEDDOES (*Washing his hands.*)
I'll tell you some hard truths, if you'll simply listen.
Born as they are, they do not understand

the principle of simple transference, this business
of heating and hammering iron, of firing bronze,
instead of which you praise, as being natural,
their barbarous ignorance of metallurgy,
of the mathematical disposition of the basic stars.
And this is not my own contempt, but science.
It is not we who are superior but they whose brain
is underaverage. The reason why they're baffled
when men like us turn into moles, mine the earth,
trace its seams of valuable metals, cover our skins
with dust, even go blind as moles inside that
valuable darkness, is not that they are closer
to sun and wind, or worship the elements,
but that they cannot make use of those elements
to drive their iron engines, make pots and kettles,
or even rifles, no more than a child could.
And that in no way should alter your affection
for their natural simplicities. The horse
is their brother, so is the wolf, and they are centaurs
on horses, wolves in war; but tell me, what horse
understands a train, what wolf, on the clearest ridge
in winter, navigates by the stars? Up to some point
an animal's instinct stops; up to the point
of the beaver's dam, the gopher's cellar, the termite's
pillars is where these first Americans are,
and, until they learn from us, are not just likely
but certain to remain. This is the truth of science.

MCLAUGHLIN

Shall I give you my own diagnosis, Jeremy?
It isn't physical. Nothing to do with the rib.
It's a question of temperament. McLaughlin
is too impulsive to be a regular major.
Let him command his Indian police. There
he can play by his own rules, like the Indians.
That's what the commission is coming to confirm.
They leave me alone, then they condemn my methods.
They give me this pompous rank to console me;
they say make decisions, but make sure we agree.
They condemn my temper by provoking it.

DR. BEDDOES

Don't worry, I'll be up there to support you.
But fighting a sergeant? That's beneath you, James.

MCLAUGHLIN

Only mud is beneath me, Jeremy. He's a man.
(CHURCH CHOIR, *off, faintly*.)
You coming to church? Someday I'll get you there.

DR. BEDDOES

Sunday is an atheist's day off. You'll be fine.

MCLAUGHLIN

I'm leaving here sicker than when I came in.
How can you be a part of the commission?

(*He exits.* DR. BEDDOES *goes to the door, watches him leave,
then clears the basin, rags, puts on his coat.*)

CHOIR (*Distant.*)

Shall we gather at the river?
The beautiful, the beautiful river?
Shall we gather at the river
That flows at the feet of the Lord?

(*Lights fade.*)

SCENE SEVEN

A church bell clangs, fades behind the next scene. TROOPERS
attend the service. MCLAUGHLIN *is pacing outside the
meetinghouse, close to the small woods. The* CONGREGATION
*enters the bare ranch house, places a white cloth on the table,
with a bowl of yellow flowers.*

JAMES EAGLE, *Indian lay preacher, enters. Behind him, his daughter* LUCY. LUCY *is Indian, in a white dress, ill-fitting.)*

EAGLE (*Reading.*)
To everything there is a time and a season. Man grows like grass and he is cut down.
(*He closes the Bible.*)
You know my daughter Lucy. I am proud that you have let her take her place humbly beside you as a true Christian soul. Her soul is in the hands of our Lord Jesus. As are all of ours. Lucy is proud that today Pastor has allowed me to make my first prayer, my first sermon with you. And those who have stayed away from this church today because our pastor announced this, I think Jesus will forgive them as he has forgiven worse. They will come to believe my faith as they will come to believe in Lucy. This is a bad time. The Ghost Dancers will be gathering. We must pray for them. We must find it in our hearts to pray for those whom we have made our enemies, so Lucy will, with your consent, lead us in this prayer, which she has learnt without my help. Lucy.

LUCY
Forgive us our trespasses as we forgive them who trespass against us. Amen.

CONGREGATION
Amen.

(BRANDON, *alone, applauds.* CATHERINE *enters, sees*
MCLAUGHLIN, *stops.*)

CATHERINE

Good morning. Why are you standing outside?

MCLAUGHLIN

Have you heard him trying to preach, Mrs. Weldon?

CATHERINE

I have heard him preach. I have heard Lucy sing.

She sings with a great deal of conviction.

Now she is engaged to Lieutenant Brandon.

She's a gift of grace. I hope he knows it.

Mrs. McLaughlin is Indian, isn't she?

Time is the difference between us and the Indians.

They think in seasons. We, we think in days.

My body, Major McLaughlin, is homesick for its rest.

Its peace.

MCLAUGHLIN

I want the same thing.

I want the same peace for Christian and Sioux.

(*In the chapel, Communion is being served.*)

CATHERINE

It is nice to talk to a man for a change.
I'm several years a widow. We're outside God's house.
You know, if I could leap the months, I'd . . .
(*Silence.*)
What did I say . . . I . . . I didn't finish. What?

MCLAUGHLIN

If you could leap the months, that you would . . .

CATHERINE

It wouldn't be the fall in 1890. It would be over.
Everything would be over. But the horror is,
we have to go by Time, the pace that Time dictates.
We can wish for it, but we cannot speed it up.
We can't catch up with Time! That's what I meant.
I meant if I were living a few months from now,
a few winters from now, even day after tomorrow,
I would have understood; even this moment here,
my talking to you outside the meetinghouse,
whatever this strange conversation means.

MCLAUGHLIN

I don't know. Well . . .

CATHERINE

Maybe I just mean to thank you for the blankets.
In the end, Major McLaughlin, what does it matter?
What does it matter in whose name we suffer?
Why, for that matter, couldn't we become Indians?
Why do the Indians have to turn into us?

MCLAUGHLIN

The man who visited you there up at the ranch,
that fellow wasn't any ghost. He come to warn you?
Sitting Bull sent him, didn't the old bullfrog?
He doesn't risk letters now, we intercept him.
So he sends not smoke up but a man of smoke.
Well, any signals he sends we can read.
That's why you stopped to talk, Mrs. Weldon.

CATHERINE

Find out what you can. Won't get no help from me.
I'm going inside. Good day, Major McLaughlin.
(MCLAUGHLIN *restrains her.*)
Will you kindly loose your fingers from my arm?

MCLAUGHLIN (*Releasing her.*)

Who'm I to come between you and your prayers?
(*He tips his hat.*)
You're still friendly with Sitting Bull. Tell me:
What message did the smoke-man bring? When

is the Ghost Dance? Oh, you smell so fresh,
Catherine. Catherine. I'll repeat it, Catherine.
Your scent is like sweet grass drying in the sun.
When will the Ghost Dancers assemble, Mrs. Weldon?
I'll call you Mrs. Weldon when I'm working,
and I'm working now. Even on the Sabbath. When?
You can prevent their massacre, not ours. Theirs.
Because . . . When?

CATHERINE
When? I'll tell you.
When roosters start laying eggs, Major McLaughlin.
When you believe in Lucy and her father.

MCLAUGHLIN
Then, as the phrase goes, Mrs. Catherine Weldon,
when that happens, it'll partly be your fault.
When the dancers turn into ghosts, remember that.
Allow me the pleasure of kissing your hand.

CATHERINE (*Extends her hand.*)
What's this authority you hope to have over me?

MCLAUGHLIN
Only the authority of pure adoration.
(*He kisses her hand.*)
It's worth more than a hundred hymns, doing that.

(*The* CONGREGATION *disperses.* LUCY *and*
BRANDON *stop.*)

CATHERINE

Lucy, I'm sorry I missed the service. I was talking
to Major McLaughlin. And the time just passed.
How are you? Congratulations to you, Lucy.

LUCY

Mrs. Weldon, I am not Lucy. My name is Swift Running
    Deer.
And that's what I feel like doing, Mrs. Weldon. Running.

BRANDON

Lucy . . . sweetheart.

LUCY

                Your friends in there, missus,
your Christian friends, don't want me with them.
Whether they . . .

CATHERINE

                Whether they do or not,
Christ loves you, Lucy. His swift running deer,
His light, light running deer, which is what Lucy means,
isn't that so? Why don't you ask Major McLaughlin here?
Doesn't Christ want Lucy for his light running deer?

(JAMES EAGLE *walks up.*)

MCLAUGHLIN

I think you'd better ask Christ, Mrs. Weldon.
His will's mysterious, Lucy, that's for sure.
(*He exits.*)

LUCY

What does Major McLaughlin mean? You're my father.
You see how they look at me in there. Answer.
Exactly what does Mr. McLaughlin mean?

EAGLE

That some doubt our conversion. You see, Lieutenant?
You see how it will be. And you, Mrs. Weldon.
You stayed outside.

CATHERINE

I had to, I'm concerned.
I was talking to Major McLaughlin about the Ghost Dance.
It had nothing to do with your preaching.

(*They begin walking.*)

BRANDON

Major McLaughlin's very haunted these days.
He has to testify to the commission.

(*They exit. A large flag descends.*)

SCENE EIGHT

The fort. A room with the flag, other Army flags, a large rug
made of blanket material is spread by DONNELLY *and*
QUINT, *unrolled onto the floor.* BRANDON *is supervising this.*
DONNELLY's *face is bruised from the fight.* DONNELLY *and*
QUINT *stand guard at either entrance, with lances.* BRANDON
spreads white notepads, some law books in a semicircle for the
commission. The SECRETARY FOR INDIAN AFFAIRS, *the*
fort commander, GENERAL, *and* DR. BEDDOES *enter.*
MCLAUGHLIN *enters, and faces the commission.* DONNELLY
proffers the Bible. CATHERINE *enters at the back.*

GENERAL

Major McLaughlin has already been sworn in.
We can take his oath as given, Sergeant Donnelly.
Let's continue where we left off yesterday.

(DONNELLY *faces* MCLAUGHLIN, *grins, then takes his place
at the entrance, after replacing the Bible.*)
That okay with you, Mr. Secretary, sir?
(*The* SECRETARY *nods.*)
With you, Dr. Beddoes?

(DR. BEDDOES *nods, withdraws a cigar case, chews on an
unlit cigar.*)

SECRETARY
Let's go carefully, Major McLaughlin.
I found yesterday's testimony very confusing.
The commission would like to remind you again
that your career is at risk here; it's clouded
by accusations that your conduct and efficiency
as the Indian agent representing the Indian Bureau
and therefore the government of the United States
has not been without prejudice, against the Sioux,
even if you have Indian police under your charge.
(*Reading notes.*)
But this is not a trial. Not a court-martial.

DR. BEDDOES
We'd all like to be sure where you stand, Jim.

GENERAL
All right, so Sitting Bull made you his proposal.

MCLAUGHLIN

He made me this proposal some months ago, sir.
I went out to see him on the Sioux Reservation
and he made me a proposal. This was the proposal.
That he and I would visit all the Indian nations.

SECRETARY

You said he told you, and here are your words:
"You do not like me, but it doesn't matter."
Is that correct, Major McLaughlin?

DONNELLY

Aha! Sorry, sir.

(*He salutes.*)

MCLAUGHLIN

That's what he said, sir.

SECRETARY

"You do not like me, but it does not matter."
What do you think that means, Major McLaughlin?

MCLAUGHLIN

It means what it says, sir, that I do not like him,
and my not liking him is of no consequence to him.
May I go on, sir? I find these interruptions—

GENERAL

They aren't interruptions, they're confirmations.
However boring or repetitious, they must be thorough.

DR. BEDDOES

Meanwhile, their conversion is spreading like the cholera
and all the nations are heading for Standing Rock
for the Ghost Dance. I understand your impatience, Jim.

MCLAUGHLIN

Thank you, Dr. Beddoes. I've never understood yours,
the amount it requires to be an Army surgeon.
(DR. BEDDOES *smiles, waves his cigar in acknowledgement.*
MCLAUGHLIN *reads.*)
He said, "You do not like me, but it doesn't matter.
We will visit all the tribes. When we reach the last one,
the one from which the idea of the Ghost Dance began,
if we do not find all the nations of the dead . . ."

SECRETARY

You mean Indians who were, are, dead.

DONNELLY

　　　　　Dead Indians, sir. The good ones.

SECRETARY (*Warning.*)

One more, Sergeant Donnelly. One more.

MCLAUGHLIN

He meant all the nations of Indians who had died.
"If we do not see them, riding on their horses,
and driving the herds of elk and buffalo,"
and he meant seeing them gazing back at us,
face-to-face, sir, in their Indian flesh resurrected,
riding with their shields and lances and families
coming back towards us from the other life,
then, he, Sitting Bull, would return to the Sioux
and tell them that the Ghost Dance was a lie.
That the resurrection in the flesh of an Indian Messiah
mounted and leading the soundless hooves
of all the dead nations, that He was a lie also.

DONNELLY (*Aside to* QUINT)

Jesus Christ. Wasn't it an ass the man rode?

GENERAL

Sergeant.

DONNELLY

Begging your pardon, sir.
I was just having an aside to Lance Corporal Quint.
But I'll keep my asides inside from now on.

SECRETARY (*To* MCLAUGHLIN)

What was your reply to his invitation, then?

MCLAUGHLIN

I couldn't travel that far to share a vision
that I'm not sure he believes in himself. I think
the Ghost Dance is a way of regathering the tribes
under his leadership. To be frank, I don't trust him.
Anyway, I said I didn't have the time or money
for such an expensive and a useless journey,
not at the expense of the Indian Bureau, sir.
I don't think apparitions are part of my duties.
I invited him to come here to the camp.
But the Ghost Dancers are afraid for his life.
They believe he has enemies in my Indian police.

SECRETARY

And here we come to the crux of my question.
Is Sitting Bull in danger from the Indian police?
And did you withhold sugar and flour from the Sioux?

MCLAUGHLIN

The agency exists for the protection of the Sioux,
not for their enslavement to our principles,
which principles are based on Christian altruism,
and if the Sioux need to be saved from the Sioux,
then the agency's job is to do it.
They accuse my men of plotting against Indians,
against their own people from the agency.
I'm afraid I don't see any betrayal, Senator.

My first responsibility is to my country,
but I don't make any distinction between
my responsibility to my country and to the Indian.
We are not betraying but protecting the Sioux
from a folly that will destroy them. If a friend
was about to put a pistol to his head, and you,
from consideration, wrenched the pistol from him,
I grant you that the interruption could be a breach
of the fellow's right to his own self-murder,
but there seems to me, as the Indian agent,
to be a more humane argument. Unless
you think that suicide is a cure
and its prevention an offence. Yes?

CATHERINE (*Rising, hand up.*)
May I ask a question?

SECRETARY
Who is she, Major McLaughlin?

MCLAUGHLIN
A friend, sir. Mrs. Weldon.

CATHERINE
A simple question?

SECRETARY

This is not—

CATHERINE

It's to Major McLaughlin.

SECRETARY

I'm afraid, Mrs. Weldon . . .

CATHERINE

Nothing to fear, sir.
It's only urgent because I have to leave now.

SECRETARY

What is the question? Make it brief, please.

CATHERINE

I'm very touched by his testimony. My question is . . .
Will you ask the major if he'll come to dinner?
I've a stew simmering. It must have boiled over.

(*Laughter.*)

MCLAUGHLIN (*To* SECRETARY)

Tell Mrs. Weldon I'd be honoured to.

SECRETARY

Major McLaughlin would be honoured to. May we proceed?
No, we'll take a recess from these distractions.

(CATHERINE *starts to exit, pauses.*)

CATHERINE

What kind of gravy with the sweet potatoes?
Never mind. You'll like it.

(*She exits. Laughter. Lights fade.*)

SCENE NINE

*The Parkin ranch, parlour. Sitting Bull's portrait hangs on
the wall.* CATHERINE *is seated with a basin in her lap,
shucking corn. Apron, shawl. Snow is blowing against the
window. High wind. A lantern sways.* CATHERINE *looks up
at the lantern.* MCLAUGHLIN *enters, a blanket on his
shoulder, closes the door.*

MCLAUGHLIN

It's gone now.

CATHERINE

What was it?

MCLAUGHLIN

Some animal down from the timber.

CATHERINE

A wolf?

MCLAUGHLIN

Here?

CATHERINE

Why not?

MCLAUGHLIN

Never seen one around here.
Did you paint this portrait?

CATHERINE

Yes, I did.
And they're hungry enough, they'll trot far, wolves.
Starvation doesn't obey geography, Major McLaughlin.
That's why you're here, though, I suppose.

MCLAUGHLIN

Why is that? Why am I here?

CATHERINE

To do what you did. Keep the wolf from the door.

MCLAUGHLIN

I've done that chore. Why did you ask me?
I'll spare you more blushing; stand by the firelight
and it'll hide the flush that comes into your face
when you speak the right answer. You asked me over.
You asked me in front of the commission.

CATHERINE

Pour yourself some whisky, Major McLaughlin.
I'll be back in the kitchen. Pretend you're home.
I heard from the woman looking after my son.
He's doing well. I couldn't leave the ranch empty.
Not with wolves and all wandering in hunger.

MCLAUGHLIN

No. And the other beasts. It's Thanksgiving.
And I thank you for your kind consideration
of inviting a grass widower over for dinner.
It would have been desolating over at the fort.
I'm extremely happy to hear about your son.

CATHERINE

When docs Mrs. McLaughlin come back, then?

MCLAUGHLIN

Whenever I send for her. It's not a good time.
Where's the whisky precisely?
    (CATHERINE *goes to a counter, bends, removes a jug,*
        places it. MCLAUGHLIN *notices the hobby horse*
            and holds it out to CATHERINE.)
This the boy's horse?

CATHERINE

Yes.

MCLAUGHLIN

I had one of these.
Ah, the imagination we had then. A stick,
a piece of rope, and the world ahead of you.
A real horse was never as real as this one.
The battles I won on these things!

CATHERINE

Just like him.
I used to watch him through the window, so
concentrated, so self-absorbed in his fancy.

MCLAUGHLIN (*Going astride it.*)

Mine was black, and he had nostrils of thunder.

I had a lance as well. Come on, Catherine, mount.

And I'll take you somewhere you've never been.

Come on, a knight and his lady. All delight,

all fancy, they go away so rapidly. Here.

CATHERINE

That's too childish.

MCLAUGHLIN

That's what's good.

Out there is a cruel world, we can escape it.

(CATHERINE *mounts behind him, holding on to his waist.*)

CATHERINE

Where are we going?

MCLAUGHLIN

Hang on now, hang on.

(*They rock together on the stick.*)

We're going to the country that has no pain.

We're riding, riding to the Land of Forgetfulness.

All the dragons are dead, all our fears are over.

(*They rock, their eyes closed several seconds.*)

In a gentle canter to the country of light.

(CATHERINE *dismounts.*)

CATHERINE

I don't trust this game. I don't trust myself.
You're a very disturbing man, James McLaughlin.
May I ask you a question?

MCLAUGHLIN

Another one? What?

(CATHERINE *goes towards the kitchen, then pauses at the
door, her back to* MCLAUGHLIN.)

CATHERINE

Would you like to go to bed before dinner?
I always found that it sharpened my appetite.

MCLAUGHLIN

That would depend on the dinner, Mrs. Weldon.

CATHERINE

I admire that. But you know what dinner is, sir,
since you're the one who brought it, from the presumption
that I was starving myself to death in sympathy
for them. So, since you know what dinner is, even if
you now don't know exactly what I am, let's go in.

MCLAUGHLIN

Go in. Go into where? Bedroom? Kitchen?

(*Silence.*)

Do you know what you and I share, Mrs. Weldon?

Do you know what quality we have in common?

(CATHERINE *turns, sits on a chair.*)

CATHERINE

Commonness?

MCLAUGHLIN

Honesty. Forthrightness.

A clarity of feelings. At least towards each other.

CATHERINE

On the contrary, sir, I've always found the opposite

to be the case. Oh, when it's some matter of strategy,

of stating our convictions and our biases,

we're blunt and vehement; I'm proud of my sharp tongue,

and you are ramrod right in your public duty,

but everything between us since our eyes met

has been oblique and sideways, not quite dishonest,

but reined in and careful. Still, it could be that

the very difference of opinion that separates us,

at least in my case, may have ignited

the low, banked fire in me.

(MCLAUGHLIN *sits on a chair, opposite her.*)

MCLAUGHLIN

      Then, that's just curiosity.
You may like to know whether the vertical man,
the ramrod officer, is the same thing horizontal.
You have eyes that char my soul, you have a passion
for justice that humiliates me. And you're right,
I'm drawn to the very thing that frightens me.

CATHERINE

What?

MCLAUGHLIN

Your cooking.

CATHERINE (*Laughing.*)

That's what killed him, then. My poor husband.

MCLAUGHLIN

Since you've turned your eyes deep into me, since
respect, which is the same as cowardice sometimes,
would have made me leave this house, and ridden back
with my head lowered, but leaving my heart behind,
thinking of the firelight edging your hair, your hands
drawing a shawl tighter or pouring me my whisky,
and done nothing about it, but imagine some excuse

when I could see you, even to talk heatedly about
the difficulty of the Indians, I want to thank you
for the incalculable honour you have paid me.

CATHERINE

Then let me go into the bedroom and draw the blind.
I'll lower the oven, but not my body's heat.
You will find it in there under a drift of quilt,
with my hair spread out, and, if you can understand,
my wedding ring next to the lamp. You'll put yours there,
out of respect; it's you who must break a contract,
the treaty you signed with your Indian wife, excuse me.
If only we were as honest with the Sioux, McLaughlin,
as I've tried to be with you. Give me five minutes.

(*She exits towards the kitchen.* MCLAUGHLIN *loosens a collar
button, then crosses to the window. He draws the curtain.*
CATHERINE *comes back from the kitchen, sees*
MCLAUGHLIN *at the window, pauses.* CATHERINE *sits
at the table.* MCLAUGHLIN *turns.*)

MCLAUGHLIN

Were you testing me? Was that some kind of sacrifice
which could ennoble you to be a victim
for the sake of your friends? You'd go to such lengths?
The length of your warm white body under a quilt,

to find out what I have found out about the Ghost Dance, after I've made love to a ghost? You'd do that to yourself? (CATHERINE *rises, begins to unbutton her dress, and enters the bedroom.* MCLAUGHLIN *returns to the window. He crosses, enters the bedroom. From offstage . . .*) I am sorry I said that. I'm sorry. I believe you.

(*Lights fade.*)

SCENE TEN

The ranch. From the riverbank, a shot. Then a shout: "Hello!" A canoe, with SARAH QUINN. *She is carrying packages.* CATHERINE *runs out to meet her.*

CATHERINE

Sarah! Sarah Quinn! What're you doing here? How's Josie? Why didn't you bring him with you?

SARAH

What've you got that's decent to eat, Kitty? Something I can sit down to with a napkin on my lap and a spray of roses in front of it? Or have you quit cookin' for yourself? Whip up something delicate, 'cause I'm tired of tearing at jerky, sourdough biscuits, and stale coffee. You look fine. Your hair shinin', your eyes bright as ever. Don't, don't hold me, I stink.

(CATHERINE *embraces her.*)

CATHERINE

Two months. How's my son, Sarah? Whyn't you bring him?

SARAH

The lad's perfectly fine where he is. Perfectly fine.

CATHERINE

Where is he? Was he strong enough for you to leave him alone down the Cannonball? Let me help you with all this baggage up to the house. So, he's well? Why didn't he come with you? Didn't he want to come?

(SARAH *hands some baggage to* CATHERINE, *then suddenly sits on the ground, her arms stretched out, her eyes closed.*)

SARAH

Smell that clean, bracing air from the pines.

(*Silence.*)

CATHERINE

There is something wrong. Oh God, I know. There is something wrong. What? What? TELL ME!

(*She sits next to* SARAH, *shaking her arm.*)

SARAH

Leave me, leave me, Kitty. Yes, there is something wrong. There's always been something wrong, and you can laugh all you like, because you're from Boston, and it's the only thing that's wrong. It will mean nothing to you when you hear it, but it's terrible, terrible.

(*Silence.*)

I've never been able to do the waltzes, to move like you, like a white birch in a breeze across the floor that carries your reflection like a lake. I'm as awkward as a buffalo with a limp. And I've come all this way up the Cannonball River for the dance at the fort, for the lanterns and the fiddles, but I am not sitting on a chair again when the elegant dancing starts. You're teaching me.

CATHERINE

He's dead, isn't he?

(*Silence.* SARAH *opens her palms, nods.* CATHERINE *moves off a far distance, near the birch trees.*)

When?

SARAH

He was perfectly fine when you left him, nearly eight weeks now, and when the grass started to change colour with the fall coming and the Cannonball was cold, the fever came back something fierce, until his whole little body felt red and brittle as a leaf, because I think, and the doctor thought, it may have been something he caught off the Sioux, maybe the cholera, 'cause he burned and burned away.

(*Silence.*)

That was two weeks ago, Kitty.

CATHERINE

Two weeks? Two whole weeks and you kept it from me, his own mother? Two weeks when I lived and cooked and prayed and went about the business of this empty ranch, and had a married man in my sheets? Then he's buried. He's buried on the banks of the Cannonball without me? Sarah Quinn?

SARAH

They were afraid of the cholera. They saw him, and once he was gone and the fever gone out like a flame, like a bright leaf with spots on it, they forced me to bury him quickly in the chapel cemetery close to the Cannonball. And I brought you his things, and I brought you his things, I brought you his things up the river, because with him gone, God, God, how I loved him, what a child. I went cold as stone, and hadn't the strength to take the trip up the river, and coming up the river, which was so lovely with the fall coming, and seeing spotted deer in the woods, I thought how hard it had been for you, Kitty Weldon, with your husband lost to the Dakotas and now a son, and yet the river was lovely, and I thought, I said what do they do, the Crow and the Sioux when their loved ones go like a season? They dance. They dance!

(CATHERINE *returns, expressionless, close to* SARAH, *silently picking up baggage and her son's things, as* SARAH *sits on the ground, rocking with grief.*)

And you'll teach me to dance, Kitty, so nothing will look so ugly again, so I can feel like a woman again, and you and me in the parlour, you'll teach me, because it is the only thing I could think of to keep me coming up the Cannonball, to do that waltz, all in white, with a fan, and my hair in a bright knot like yours, and the punch bowl and the fiddles playing. Will you teach me a few delicate steps? For his sake?

CATHERINE

Yes, if you want to, Sarah. Come into the house.

(*They move into the parlour.* CATHERINE *opens the box with the lace dress, fits it against* SARAH.)

SARAH

That other box is his things. Oh, Kitty, Kitty.

(CATHERINE *pins up her hair, picks up a kitchen fan, then indicates that* SARAH *should sit.* CATHERINE *goes to the centre of the room. Takes a pose.*)

CATHERINE

Now, pay close attention. This is the first position for the quadrille. We'll do the mazurka, and the polka next. Delicately now, watch me; the right foot is delicately extended, delicately, tell that to Sergeant Donnelly. So stand up, Sarah, and do as I do. Then the fiddles strike up, but slowly . . .

(SARAH *rises reluctantly, following* CATHERINE*'s lead.*)

And a one, then a two . . . Did he suffer, Sarah, did my little boy suffer, then a turn, ah, that's right, now the gentleman's arm, and . . .

(SARAH *collapses in her arms.* CATHERINE *holds her.*)

Like them, nothing must prevent us from dancing. Let's learn that from them. Straighten up, arm out, Sarah. Arm out!

(*Music begins, slow fiddles. Lights fade.*)

SCENE ELEVEN

The fort. A punch table with fruit, food, cakes, a banner marked HAPPY ANNIVERSARY, FORT BRILL, *music on*

track, FIDDLERS, *and* COUPLES *dancing at the church
social.* JAMES EAGLE, LUCY *in her white dress, not dancing,
leaning against a wall alone. The* FIDDLERS *strike up a
polka, and the* OFFICERS *and* LADIES *stomp and whirl and
hoot in the growing speed of the dance.* JAMES EAGLE *comes
to dance with* LUCY, *but* LUCY *declines. He insists, but* LUCY
shakes her head, near tears. Her father moves away. The
GENERAL *enters and looks on. The polka finishes.*
DONNELLY *comes towards* LUCY.

DONNELLY

Ladies and gentlemen of Fort Brill. This is a Christian social, and we're glad to have officers and gentlemen and their
ladies with us. We are glad to have Lucy with us. We want
to make folks like Lucy feel at home in good Christian company, and so I am going to ask Lucy to dance.

(*Applause.*)

Wait, wait. I am going to ask Lucy to dance, but I am going to
ask Lucy, whose name in the other way of life, I believe, was
Swift Running Deer, to dance *alone.* To show us not whether she
has learnt our square dances as well as her Bible, but to show us
how we too can dance the common celebration of life. Lucy?

(*Silence. Then to* JAMES EAGLE, *who nods.*)

With your permission, padre? Lucy. Could you show us that
you haven't forgotten the old dance? Would you do a few
steps for us, Swift Running Deer? We need drums and clapping. Drums, war drums. Because out there, the Sioux and

the Dakotas are getting ready to do their own steps, and
we'd better learn them, hadn't we, General? So, join me will
you, to this beat? To this beat, Swift Running Deer.

(DONNELLY *begins clapping and laughing; the others join in.*
LUCY *moves to go out, but* DONNELLY *blocks her. He does his*
version of a war dance to laughter and hooting, and LUCY
lifts up her dress and, with a rage that builds into a frenzy of
movement, screams, hoots, and sobs to the clapping, as
CATHERINE *enters.* CATHERINE *crosses, collects* LUCY.
Silence. CATHERINE *consoles* LUCY.)

CATHERINE

God save us all from your Christian charity.
(*She leads* LUCY *out.* JAMES EAGLE *follows. Then the*
fiddlers resume, and the whirling polka.)
Lucy?

LUCY

No more Lucy. I can't give you a name.
My dad doesn't like me to talk in the old way.
But I think I know what I would call you.

CATHERINE

What?

(BRANDON *comes out.*)

LUCY

"The Bright Hair Who Loved Us." Is that good?

CATHERINE

That is my inner, my secret, my heart's name.

"Bright Hair Who Loved Us." Loved? Loves. Loves.

(*She embraces* LUCY, *who keeps still.*)

And until it turns into grey ashes like the fire,

that will be Catherine Weldon's name, ah, child!

Lucy, I'll tell you this. I had a son.

When I felt too dispirited to cook,

not wanting to eat because the child's tongue was swollen,

his throat so raw, I would boil berries,

deny, starve myself. That was easy, Lucy,

because my body was starving with the Sioux.

Sioux-stew I used to call it, gulping air.

Making my meals from berries and from bark.

A wolf, when it is starving, eats the wind.

I am an Indian, without an Indian name.

Christen me. No unchristen me. Give me a name.

What name would you give me, Miss Lucy Running Deer?

LUCY

"Bright Hair Who Loves Us." Not Catherine.

Bright Hair Who Loves Us. Goodbye.

(*To* BRANDON)

No. Don't come with me. I'm going home.

(*She runs off.*)

CATHERINE

Leave her alone. These things take time.

(*Lights fade. Music off.* DONNELLY *is pushed on by a raging* SARAH.)

SARAH

Patrick Donnelly, I didn't come all the way up the Cannonball River with a lace dress in a box to watch you make a drunken disgrace of yourself.

(*She shakes him, throws him down.*)

DONNELLY

Jesus, Mary, and Joseph, I meant no offence by it. Have you lost your sense of humour, woman? And what's there in her own dancin' to be ashamed of? Did I tell you you're like an angel in that outfit?

(*He rises, collapses, rises.*)

I'm on my knees, Sarah, and since I'm here, I might as well propose. Will you take my hand in holy matrimony, till death do us part? There's battle in the air, the heathen tribes are gatherin', and we've little time.

SARAH

I'd rather go out in that wilderness again, Patrick Donnelly, facing bears and blizzards and the naked heathen, that's my answer. And with Mrs. Weldon so quiet though she just had to suffer the death of her son.

DONNELLY

I didn't know that. I had no knowledge of that.

SARAH

I'm going back down the Cannonball tomorrow. I'm taking her there to see him, at least where he lies.

DONNELLY

I'd no knowledge of that, I swear. No knowledge at all.

SARAH

You've no knowledge of anything, least of all human feelings, especially any woman's, and yet I wish you safety in battle; but don't follow me. I'm away.

DONNELLY

Come back, Sarah, the dancin's just begun.
(SARAH *exits.* DONNELLY *follows a few steps,*
staggers. Stops.)
You'll come back up the river to me. You'll come back up the Cannonball to your beloved Patrick.
(*He waits, heads back towards the dancing, stops, cups his hand to his mouth and does a long coyote yelp. Lights fade.*)

SCENE TWELVE

The Reservation, an open space. Dusk. The GHOST
DANCERS, SIOUX, *other* INDIANS, *wearing black hats low on
their foreheads, blankets around their clothes, whose cut is a
mixture of Indian and Western. They cover themselves with
handfuls of snow (flour) and squat in a circle, humped over,
their backs to us, in silence.*
KICKING BEAR *enters, leading* LUCY. LUCY *'s face is painted
white, with a few markings. Her dress Sioux. The* GHOST
DANCERS *hum.* KICKING BEAR *stands in front of them, lifts*
LUCY, *swirls her around several times, then sets her down.*
BRANDON, *in black hat, his face marked, enters, crouched,
and sits among the* GHOST DANCERS.

KICKING BEAR

Our daughter Swift Running Deer has returned.
(*Chanting.*)
"*My children, take this road.
My children, go this way,*"
Says the Wanekia.

GHOST DANCERS

"It is a good, good road,"
Says the Wanekia.

KICKING BEAR (*Spinning* LUCY *around.*)
The whole world of the dead is returning, returning.
Our nation is coming, is coming.
The spotted eagle brought us the message
Bearing the father's word.
The word and the wish of the father.
Over the glad new earth they are coming.
Our dead come, driving the elk and the deer.
See them hurrying the herds of buffalo.

(LUCY *lets out a loud, long, possessed wail.* KICKING BEAR
puts his hand over her forehead. LUCY *threshes, moans, emits
another possessed wail, begins to dance slowly.* BRANDON
hurls away his blanket.)

BRANDON

LUCY!
(*He tries to move towards her. The* GHOST DANCERS *reach
out and grasp his ankles. He falls; one sits on his feet.
He struggles.*)
LUCY! THIS IS MADNESS.
LUCY! PAY ATTENTION TO ME.

LUCY, FOR CHRIST'S SAKE.

For Jesus Christ's sake.

I came out here to take you home.

Lucy, please! Please, if you love me!

I love you, Swift Running Deer.

(LUCY *dances, even if she hears him.* GHOST DANCERS *take*
BRANDON *away, shouting and cursing.*)

KICKING BEAR (*Chanting.*)

Our dead come driving the elk and the deer.

See them hurrying the herds of the buffalo.

(*The* GHOST DANCERS *who evicted* BRANDON *return, take
their places.* BRANDON *reappears farther off, watching* . . .)

GHOST DANCERS (*Seated, chanting.*)

This the father has promised.

This the father has given.

(KICKING BEAR *is transfixed, arms extended, crucified.*
LUCY, *crying, chanting in Sioux, dances. Lights fade.*)

ACT TWO

SCENE ONE

The fort. The Army mess. DR. BEDDOES *finishes playing a chess game with* BRANDON *to the applause of* THREE YOUNG OFFICERS.

DR. BEDDOES

Gentlemen, I'm never too happy about victory.
I was with Custer at the Little Big Horn,
but it wasn't that victory that embittered me.
I was never a military man.

BRANDON
> That much we know, sir.

(*Laughter.*)

DR. BEDDOES
Most victories are a burden on the victor.

They have to nurse, to feed and shelter their captives,

according to the basic courtesies of war,

so if one victory brings in a thousand prisoners,

the cost is to the captor who adopts them,

who, if he is civilised, will give them doctors,

share his expensive medicine with his own wounded,

feed them, barrack them in his humanity.

Perhaps in the long run we saved a lot of money

by losing the Battle of the Little Big Horn.

Our country owes far more to Armstrong Custer,

gentlemen, than you're prepared to give him credit for.
> (*A sarcastic groan from* OFFICERS.)
The man had vision in his sense of thrift.

Whereas the Indian . . .
> (MCLAUGHLIN *enters.* DR. BEDDOES *pauses. The* OFFICERS
> *watch* MCLAUGHLIN.)
You're late for our game, Jim; whereas the Indian,

who has a sharper sense of husbandry,

saves himself the trouble. He collects scalps.

He mutilates the dying enemy, when there are wounded
he sends his women and boys to chop them up,
while we use surgeons. The women play with the heads.
This I have witnessed through these very spectacles,
which I now cloud with my breath and rub with my kerchief
and replace over weary eyes that pray never again
to see those barbaric deformities of men like you
dumped on that butcher block of a field hospital.
To me, they are all embodied in Sitting Bull.
I think James shares my hatred. Don't you, McLaughlin?

(MCLAUGHLIN, *uniform loosened, comes over from the basin
where he has been washing up, carrying a jug of corn liquor.*)

MCLAUGHLIN

You're a frustrated senator, Dr. Beddoes.
Are you trying to frighten these Army gentlemen?
Yeah. I have no respect whatever for that fat whore,
that tun of grease, but if you had thousands of warriors
behind you, who couldn't be a great leader?
She knew him in Colonel Cody's circus.
You must read a pamphlet I wrote, a little thing
but an honest one, called "My Friend the Indian."

BRANDON

You sold me one, Major.

MCLAUGHLIN

I've a thin salary.

(*Laughter. Sarcastic groans.*)

BRANDON

Did you read it, Doctor?

DR. BEDDOES

It is a fair piece of work.

Fair in the sense of its justice, not its style.

MCLAUGHLIN

What's wrong with its style? No, please don't, Doctor!

DR. BEDDOES

It matches its geography, Major McLaughlin,

it is plain prose written on a Great Plain.

MCLAUGHLIN

A senator. A senator. A disappointed Demosthenes.

A humanitarian who despises mankind.

DR. BEDDOES

You despise your subject, too. Sitting Bull.

MCLAUGHLIN

Because he is crafty, avaricious, mendacious,
and ambitious, with all the faults of an Indian
and none of their nobler virtues. That's in the book.

BRANDON

Dr. Beddoes denies them any virtues at all.
That's a contradiction of what Lucy is.

MCLAUGHLIN

Dr. Beddoes would deny them medicine if he could.
But we're both bound to an oath.

DR. BEDDOES

                   In the smallpox epidemic,
in the plague that took thousands and thousands
because some Mandan brought it here in a blanket,
I gave soldier and enemy my complete attention.
I have never failed to. You have a question, sir?

BRANDON

Aren't you damned tired fighting Indians, Doctor?

DR. BEDDOES

I'm going to sound like Ulysses in the camp
talking to exhausted captains in the faded tents,

and the sagging causes seven years into a war
that was turning into an embittered expedition.
It was not the piled bodies that defeated them,
not the smoke or the carnage, but a quiet period
like this; when meditation paralysed the officers,
when the reflecting fire on their bronzed faces
with a Myrmidon plucking at some instrument—
the smoke drifted from the fire that was its home
the way you soldiers, you officers and gentlemen,
in such intervals brood on silence, not only
on the long war, but on this fact. Which truth?
Life. Life is a virulent, pernicious cell
that, from the moment I have watched it form,
worries and wars with itself towards extinction.
It is like the signal curling from this cigar,
a furious ember that delights as it consumes
the pleasure that it gives me. It is a body
burning towards ash, like the coming autumn
that fires the sumac with autumnal strokes,
and there is nothing like these intervals from war
along these plains, and this goes for the Indians
when they have lowered their lances and
hung up their shields, to see that bright disease
for what it is, especially, if like me,
you have wiped an apron rusty with young men's blood,
and walked out from the buckets and bandages
to step out and look up at the peaceful stars,

then see them as virulent and tenacious cells
riddling the night sky over the Dakotas.
Then, if they are bodies, they are not heavenly
but doomed to life, just as we are, gentlemen,
no matter how long their span, how slow their arc,
so many innumerable cigar ends burning,
in spite of which you turn back into the tent,
back to the wounded, the horrible lacerations,
drawing a new resolution for what is too familiar
to be despair. And your oath is renewed
as wearily as that dawn on the Trojan shore,
like the lances of reeds lifted along the water.
Men make war to avoid death, or to bring it closer
to an inevitable end. Sometimes, when I'm tired,
I see the ghosts of Indian faces at the window
wanting to be let in, to get nearer the fire.

    (*Pauses. An Indian face appears at the window.* KICKING
        BEAR's. *He shakes off the hallucination.*)

And I'm much too tired to let them in. But
if I did, if I did, gentlemen, and passed out cigars
to all their chiefs and the braves, there'd be one fact,
one fact in common. Not merely that we die,
but because of the helpless treachery of that cell
that brightens and extinguishes all of us.
For which, as a surgeon, I offer no solution,
and for which I won't advance a mystery.
The peroration ends here. Go out and fight,

and fight with all the fury you can summon.

After this lecture, you'll earn my admiration,

and something pretty close to envy, even.

Go out and do your job, and I'll do mine.

And let the enemy do his also. My cigar is cold.

> (*He relights it, looking at* MCLAUGHLIN.)

What do you think, Major McLaughlin? Too cynical.

Too long, perhaps. Life is a very long answer

to a simple question.

MCLAUGHLIN

What do I think?

I think you're a corruption. I think disease

like this, this tired doctor's talk

is damned dangerous, if not close to treason.

Thank God your hand doesn't shake. Not yet.

I think you drink too much and talk too much.

You're our biggest risk: an atheistic surgeon.

The Indian believes without doubt. Doubt

is what your diseased advice can undo

for the morale of the Army. I think, Doctor,

that though you're officially on the Army's side,

you're Sitting Bull's best friend. I believe

the stars in heaven are not cells but angels.

DR. BEDDOES

Are what?

MCLAUGHLIN

Angels. The eyes of them.

The lights of them. The blessed sacredness of them.

That's what I see when I stop my horse at night

crossing the Plains. Not dying cigar butts

but travelling souls, like the far lanterns of wagons.

None of what you said in front of those boys,

who aren't soldiers yet, none of that despair

would come from the Indian. They are incapable

of blasphemy. Of science. Of civilisation.

But I guess they'll pick up that infection

you been preachin', until it's wide as the cholera,

and the tribes fall down and die like yellow leaves

poisoned by your cigar smoke, and much faster

than the repeating rifle. It's a fine night.

I'll go outside and inhale more poison.

DR. BEDDOES

Wait.

(MCLAUGHLIN *waits.*)

Mrs. McLaughlin's what's called a Christian squaw.

You must be in a terrible conflict, you poor man.

Married to an enemy as our Indian agent.

No wonder when you stop your horse at night

you see the stars as angels not cigar butts.

If my wife were an Indian, I'd need to see them, too.

It's just a philosophical discussion, Jim.

(*Sound of hooves. It stops. A face appears at the window:*
JAMES EAGLE.)

BRANDON

There's a trap and some people outside.
I'll get it, Major McLaughlin.

(*He opens the door.* EAGLE, *the Indian preacher, stands in
the doorway.*)

EAGLE

Dr. Beddoes. Come please. My daughter hang herself.
(*To* MCLAUGHLIN)
Lucy. You remember Lucy. Swift Running Deer.
My daughter, Major McLaughlin. She hang herself.

(BRANDON *runs outside.* DR. BEDDOES *does not move, his
head lowered.*)

MCLAUGHLIN

Where, where did she do this? Is she still alive? Where?

DR. BEDDOES

Hanged is the past tense in plain English, James.
You can hear from his agitation that she's dead.
And that one is beyond my profession, the resurrection
is in others' hands, not mine.

MCLAUGHLIN

Jesus Christ, man. Jesus.

DR. BEDDOES

My words exactly. Where is your daughter, friend?

(*He goes over to* EAGLE.)

EAGLE

She is outside, on the trap with Mrs. Weldon.

Mrs. Weldon wanted to stay with her. She sent me in.

She is out there, in the street, in the trap

like a sack of flour. I'll show you, Doctor.

DR. BEDDOES

NO, DON'T SHOW ME. DON'T YOU KNOW WHEN

SOMEBODY'S DEAD?

And I don't want McLaughlin bringing her in here.

She's your responsibility, Preacher, not mine.

There's nothing I can do about her. What?

What do you want me to do, pass my spectacles

over her mouth and see if her breath mists them,

so that you can clutch at a feather? Ghosts

don't breathe. Do not bring me any more dead.

Do not bring her in here. This is an Army post.

She's a civilian corpse. Go away, McLaughlin.

(MCLAUGHLIN *exits, then returns with* CATHERINE.)

CATHERINE

She rode out to talk to me on the Parkin ranch.
I gave her tea and biscuits. She seemed settled.
She told me she wanted to grow her hair out again.
She said that after that madness at the church social
when Sergeant Donnelly had forced her to dance,
she wanted to go back, in spite of her father,
to being what she was. I said that she should.
She stroked my hair. She said it was like corn.
We walked by the creek and she chattered like it,
saying how she really believed. And she was shining
and talkative like the creek in the sunshine.
And I waved goodbye to her, lifting my apron.
And that was my last of Lucy, Swift Running Deer.
I hate the sight of every one of you.

EAGLE

She came home. I was at church. When I came home
she was hanging from a tree behind the cabin.
I cut her down. I believed she was still breathing.
I wanted to believe it. I made her breathe.
I put my own pulse in her, I lent her my heart.
Then I folded her over the horse and I rode out,
God knows why, out to the ranch, to Mrs. Weldon.

DR. BEDDOES

Why Mrs. Weldon, why not to a doctor first?
Or a medicine man. Why Mrs. Weldon?
Do you want me to perform a resurrection?
I don't have the required instruments or the faith.

MCLAUGHLIN

Doctor. Dr. Beddoes.

DR. BEDDOES

You've seen dead Indians.
So have we all, I've seen hundreds of them.
The report is an Army form, I can't fill it out.
It's for the military. You knew that, Mrs. Weldon.
I know why you brought her here. But listen,
I know you weren't expecting any miracles.
You brought her here to show us what we have done.
That's barbarous, Mrs. Weldon. That is cruel.
Please.

BRANDON (*Outside.*)

Lucy! Oh, God in heaven, my Lucy! Lucy!
I'm sorry!

CATHERINE

I hope I didn't, Dr. Beddoes.

I hoped there was time enough to do something.

I'm sorry.

EAGLE

It is okay, it is okay.

This must be to you a stupid expedition.

We hope beyond hope you could revive her.

(EAGLE *exits.* CATHERINE *stands at the door, spits,*
then exits.)

MCLAUGHLIN

Catherine! Don't ride off. Catherine, wait!

A horse. Trooper! Get me a horse, Donnelly!

(*He exits.*)

DR. BEDDOES (*At the window.*)

It's clearing up. I thought there'd be more snow.

(*Sound of a trap moving off.*)

I didn't invent death, you know. He did.

(*He looks up. Lights fade.*)

SCENE TWO

The parlour, the Parkin ranch. CATHERINE. *Sound of hooves.*
MCLAUGHLIN *crashes in, slams the door.*

CATHERINE

Faith. It killed Lucy. Faith killed Swift Running Deer.
She paid the price of that difference.

MCLAUGHLIN

My wife converted, and it didn't kill her.

(*He tears down Sitting Bull's portrait. They fight over it.*
MCLAUGHLIN *gives it up.*)

CATHERINE

Your wife is dead. You just haven't noticed.
Her heart is dead. She is among the lifeless.
They all are. They knew they were already ghosts.

MCLAUGHLIN

Was that why you took me to your bed, Mrs. Weldon?
Was that why you prepared that dinner, in which,

if I was the damned turkey, I must now say thanks,

because your legs were hoisted over the linen

with your hair shaken out, making it an altar

of some sacrifice for the heathen? Wasn't it

because you wanted me to tell you what stratagems

the Army had to prepare for the Ghost Dance?

What was all that prolonged admiration

you pretended for me, a man married to one of them?

My wife wouldn't have dared to ask me.

She would not have lied to me with her body.

That was more than adultery. It was blasphemous.

CATHERINE

Blasphemous. I did it in good faith.

MCLAUGHLIN

        Good faith. Aye.

Whose? Yours? The Indians? In whose good faith?

Because they're damned different, as you know.

CATHERINE

What exactly are you accusing me of?

I have lost a husband, a son. A friend. What?

MCLAUGHLIN

I'm not accusing you, I'm asking a question.

CATHERINE

What I did I did in my body's faith.

But honesty may be a different thing from faith.

I did it not from loneliness, although that, too,

but because I felt my longing was not sin,

but because I might have been the wife you needed,

and God forgive me for being forthright, McLaughlin,

or for sounding as if I felt your wife unworthy

of you because she is Indian. I was in love.

And that was the penalty I had for siding with them.

God punished me with that love. But now it's dead.

I killed it in bed with my body, Major McLaughlin.

I coarsened it with lust. I drove it on,

I thrashed in those sheets so that when it was over

I could sweat out my disgust.

MCLAUGHLIN

You regret what happened in that room?

CATHERINE

With all my heart. With my body especially.

I scalded it, I rubbed it all over with ashes

in a tub, I scoured it as if it had caught the plague.

MCLAUGHLIN

Oh, I thank you.

CATHERINE

You thank me? For what?

MCLAUGHLIN

For your blanket, from which I caught the cholera.
I caught love's plague. I walk around in a fever;
there is a lantern in my body, people can see through
my ribs like a leaf in the light, and, Catherine,
that leaf is scratched with your name. I am saying,
without any more fancy, that I love you now.

CATHERINE

I thought of you coming back up the Cannonball.
But perhaps the anger and the disgust I felt
as I scoured myself was the rage that you confided
nothing to me about the Army's decisions.
Something I could pass on to the Indians.
That I had not dissolved you enough,
that your melting was only partial.
That my body was out of practice, perhaps.
And that if you had been thoroughly satisfied,
you would have answered those questions I put gently
to you. But you confided nothing.

MCLAUGHLIN

                    I still know nothing.
But if I had then, I doubt I would have told you.

CATHERINE

Lucy. My husband. My young, buried boy!
One body is not enough for you, you want thousands
as well as mine, lying out there in the sheets
of a dead winter. My love is a ghost now, you hear?
It died in those sheets. Well, that was my Ghost Dance,
that thrashing about in the linen.

MCLAUGHLIN

That is a lie. Look,
look at your face in this mirror, the cheeks; look,
they're firelit without a fire. You still love me.

CATHERINE

God punish me, Major McLaughlin.
(*Pause.*)
But yes I do.

MCLAUGHLIN

Major McLaughlin: you talk like an Irish chambermaid
when you get formal. Then sit down, Catherine,
and I'll tell you. I'll tell you the Army's plans.
I'll tell you secrets to redeem their deaths.

CATHERINE

It's too late. I don't want to hear. Too late.
I came to this place too late. I loved you too late.

It is too late for us to change sides,
too late for me to get out of the Irish habit
of calling you Major McLaughlin with my clothes on.

MCLAUGHLIN

The Army plans to leave the fort abandoned,
with that appearance at least, so the Sioux
can ride into the gate . . .

CATHERINE

An ambush? I don't want . . .
I don't want to hear it. Do what you have to do.
I thought I could change things, but I can't.

MCLAUGHLIN

Then when the gate is breached, the soldiers—

CATHERINE

It is too late to warn them, I don't want to hear.
(*She puts her hands over her ears and runs outside,
screaming.*)
I DON'T WANT TO HEAR IT. THERE'S NOTHING I
CAN DO.
(MCLAUGHLIN *takes up his hat and cloak and goes out.*
CATHERINE *is sitting in the snow, her face lifted.*
MCLAUGHLIN *comes up, stands behind her, at some distance.*

CATHERINE *does not turn, speaking softly.*)
Let me tell you, such a white, wide, and wonderful peace
will cover these plains, that before my hair is white,
it will cover everything with God's silence.
That is what I look forward to now, James.

MCLAUGHLIN
So do we all, Catherine. So do we all.
    (*He puts on his hat and cape; comes and stands in
        front of her.*)
Open your eyes. Don't close your eyes on me.
What I did, or did not do, I did from an oath.
I did it in the conviction that I was helping,
not trying to destroy. For God's sake, open your eyes.
Thank you. Look long and clearly. What they see
is a man who worships you. Print that image there,
let it be like a mirror that keeps his body;
give that mirror a memory. Give that mirror a voice
that can echo like a rifle over the Dakotas.
The Indian agent loved the widow at the Parkin ranch.
  (*Again, he walks off a few steps, then returns. He removes a
    folded letter from his pocket, breaks the seal, opens the
      envelope, lets the letter drop at* CATHERINE*'s knees.*)
There are my sealed orders, which I have opened
and sealed again. They contain, in great detail,
with a map, with positions and times, with placements,

the deployment of cavalry and the Indian scouts,
what the Army intends. This is not treachery.
Take it, it can save thousands of lives.
If they call it treachery, well, so be it.

(*He walks away.* CATHERINE *looks at the order, then slowly
picks it up. Slowly, she tears it, staring in the distance. A far
bugle. Then the sound of* MCLAUGHLIN*'s horse. A whinny,
then a canter, then a fading gallop.* CATHERINE *picks up the
pieces of the letter, spreads them out on the snow in front of
her, then she scrapes up the pieces carefully and puts them
into her bodice. She exits. Lights fade.*)

SCENE THREE

Fade in immediately. The ranch. Three days later.
CATHERINE *goes to the door, returns inside. She sits on a
rocker, rocking back and forth. Stands, stops the rocker. Goes
to the door. She cups her hands to her mouth and gives three
quick, hollow hoots. Silence. She goes to the rocker. She lifts the
rocker and places it in the open door where she can look at the
woods.* KICKING BEAR *appears. He is wearing a stovepipe hat
with feathers, an oversized army coat. He is drunk. He stands*

where he stood before, swaying. CATHERINE *claps her hands.*
He does not turn. Suddenly he collapses, folding, and squats in
the snow. CATHERINE *goes up to him.*

CATHERINE

Did you give Sitting Bull the letter? The plan.
Did you show him McLaughlin's plan?

KICKING BEAR

I showed him the Army plan. I showed him.
I have a new hat.

CATHERINE

Yes. I see that.
Who gave it to you? The hat. Who gave it to you?
They got you drunk? The patrol.

KICKING BEAR

The soldiers. The soldiers gave me the hat.
Sergeant Donnelly. We drink, we drunk.

CATHERINE

And they gave you whisky. Whisky and a hat.
What did Sitting Bull say when you showed him?
When you showed Sitting Bull the plan, did he understand?
Did you explain what I told you to explain?

KICKING BEAR

They gave me the whisky first and then the hat.

Sitting Bull said that it is too late.

They are going ahead with the Ghost Dance.

In spite of Colonel Cody. It will not be the circus.

(*He removes the hat, polishes it.*)

This is the hat of the President. Soldiers said.

He said that the tribes were ready. No change.

Then the whisky. Then they told me to come here.

Then they told me to come back to the fort.

But nothing will change. I go back to the fort.

CATHERINE

And the soldiers ambushed you drunk and took the plans,

the plans that had Major McLaughlin's name on it?

KICKING BEAR

Yes. And now I must go back to the fort. More whisky.

They gave me their word, and I gave them mine.

My horse is drunk. The whole world is drunk.

The soldiers are waiting for me. Up in the pines.

(*He rises, singing, puts the hat on, exits. Lights fade.*)

SCENE FOUR

A cell in the fort. Long shadows, from the cell bars. KICKING BEAR, MCLAUGHLIN, DR. BEDDOES, *and a bottle of whisky. A chair, table.* DONNELLY *waiting.*

KICKING BEAR

Sergeant Donnelly is my very good friend.

DONNELLY

Yes, sir. We had a bit of a jar together.
It's our common bond with the heathen, is it not?

KICKING BEAR

I hold in my hand a cold piece of the morning star.
I was carried that high by the whirlwind I made
by dancing the Ghost Dance.

DR. BEDDOES

You were carried up there
by exhaustion, by fatigue.

(*To* MCLAUGHLIN)

Fatigue. Starvation.

Hallucinations brought on by a lack of blood
in the brain.

(*To* KICKING BEAR)

Give me the stone from the star.

(KICKING BEAR *gives him the stone.* DR. BEDDOES *passes it
to* MCLAUGHLIN.)

You recognise the mineral. Quartz. Nothing.

MCLAUGHLIN (*To* KICKING BEAR)

You know you are forbidden to dance the Ghost Dance.
This piece of stone is nothing. You went to the star.
Tell Dr. Beddoes and me what you saw on the star.
Tell us, Kicking Bear, and you can have more whisky.

DR. BEDDOES

Don't let him get unintelligible. If he's drunk,
and you add drunkenness to the memory of delirium,
we'll have that madness I hate. Possession.
There'll just be more of that spiritual garbage
that people call vision.

(MCLAUGHLIN *holds up his hand.*)

All right, I'm sorry.

Your examination is your job. Go ahead.
But no more whisky yet.

MCLAUGHLIN
Kicking Bear, listen.

KICKING BEAR
You listen. And believe when you listen. There,
I spoke to the dead. I lay on the ground. Three days.

DR. BEDDOES
Beginning, middle, and end. Always three days.
There is that one metre common to every myth.
Three days. No different from the Resurrection.

KICKING BEAR
Three days on the ground, without eating,
without drinking, without moving, without . . .

DR. BEDDOES
                                        Without any reason.
Starving, dehydrating themselves, to become ghosts.
It would be interesting to find out, McLaughlin,
if those who rolled away the stone from the tomb
had had any breakfast and were on a strict diet.
The dance is a corruption of the Christian fable
which they have seized and altered. There's a Messiah,
when they never had one before. An Indian Messiah,
the same as Aryans have seized Christ from the Semites,
which, by the way, was a desert religion. A landscape

given to the body heat of mirages, a landscape
of stones wriggling in heat waves without water.

MCLAUGHLIN

That may be so, but you're maligning my faith.
The desert is your own emptiness, Jeremy.

DR. BEDDOES

Then you and that man there believe the same thing.
I'm sure to you Christ has an Irish accent.
Why don't you call him McChrist? The same way
Kicking Bear has his own name for Him.
He's as parched as one of the desert fathers.
Give him another shot of the Irish, Donnelly.

(DONNELLY *pours a shot of whisky, hands it to* KICKING
BEAR, *then pulls it away.*)

MCLAUGHLIN

What have we done to these people's minds?

(*Silence.* KICKING BEAR *reaches for the shot glass.*
DONNELLY *pours him another drink.*)

DR. BEDDOES

What have we done? We have taught them doubt.

MCLAUGHLIN

Taught them doubt. And that's a good thing, man?

DR. BEDDOES

Doubt is the foundation of enquiry, enquiry
proceeds to search, and search is science,
and science is the dissolution of shadows.
Even the scientist is sceptical of the achievements
of science. Not like you believers. We believe in doubt.

MCLAUGHLIN

Kicking Bear, did Mrs. Weldon give you this plan?

(*He shows* KICKING BEAR *the orders.*)

KICKING BEAR

Yes. Mrs. Weldon.
Bright Hair Who
Loves the Sioux!

(*He rises, pours himself another shot glass, gives one to*
DONNELLY, *who declines. Then he begins to sing, softly, then
louder: "Rock of Ages."*)

DR. BEDDOES

There's your faith. Look at the dilation of the pupils.

KICKING BEAR (*As a* GHOST DANCER.)

And what about our tribe? Speak, in me what?

Tell me the voice that lives inside me, what will happen?

(*The voice inside, changing* . . .)

They will know the rapture of exaltation,

the feathers in their hair will make them eagles

over the broken mountains; the lakes will enter

and prickle their cold skins like the fishes;

they will tire like the salmon of a ladder of stones,

and not only the Sioux, not only the Sioux,

the Arapahos, the Cheyennes, the Brules, the Ogalalas,

to the drum in the heart, before the wide silence.

MCLAUGHLIN

Take him away, Donnelly. Put him in the cell.

DR. BEDDOES

I haven't finished questioning him.

MCLAUGHLIN

                        Take him off, Sergeant.

(*To* DR. BEDDOES)

You look clouded. Something worrying you?

Something the matter? Talk to me, Jeremy.

(DONNELLY *takes* KICKING BEAR *off.*)

DR. BEDDOES

How else could Kicking Bear acquire the plan,
except there was someone in the Indian police
who told it to him?

MCLAUGHLIN

My men are trustworthy.

DR. BEDDOES

Then how did Mrs. Weldon acquire that knowledge?
Carnally?

MCLAUGHLIN

Could be Sergeant Donnelly.
He's got a mouth as wide as the Cannonball River.
Carnally? Wash your mouth, Jeremy.

DR. BEDDOES

What do I mean? Come on,
the woman's face glows when she speaks to you,
her heart shines like light through an army tent.
That's what happened, isn't it?

(*Silence.*)

MCLAUGHLIN

Well, what's your next move, Jeremy? What next?
To write me up like a medical report? Listen.
I can see what Catherine argues about the Sioux.

DR. BEDDOES

You're a lone wolf, James. And you know what a wolf does,
how it stakes out its territory. It lifts its hind leg,
at different points, in a circle, to warn intruders.
But here you run with the pack, and that's the Army;
but maybe you've staked the fences at the Parkin ranch
only to protect what's likely to betray you.
Lifting your leg won't do it, excuse the image,
but there's something too primal, too pungent
in your conduct. Besides, you're a married man.

MCLAUGHLIN

But only to an Indian, no? You don't think that counts.
Not around here. I thought you would be happy
that I have returned to the pack, as you call it,
and sniffed out the right mate.

DR. BEDDOES

                   She's a lovely woman.
But spare me the horror of being in love with her.
Don't you have any respect for our exhaustion

from fighting, for mine with being an Army surgeon,
that a woman should excite you? Sitting Bull's pet?

MCLAUGHLIN

I should crack your jaw. You talk too dirty.

DR. BEDDOES

My hands are dirty, James, not only my mouth.
From buckets and rewashed bandages, from dead boys
on butcher tables. My mouth can't help it.
My eyes can't help it. They're tired of the field.
That woman still sees the Sioux as maligned angels;
she never stood up among their atrocities.

MCLAUGHLIN

I have and you know it. I stood with you in the field.

DR. BEDDOES

But the field has faded, and the smell of a fresh body
is making you forget it. That pleasant scent
is making your oblivion. Of us. Of your duty.

MCLAUGHLIN

I do my duty.

DR. BEDDOES

But treachery is exciting.

That excitement in betrayal, that's adultery.

(MCLAUGHLIN *slaps him.*)

That's a confession. And the end of my concern.

(*They watch each other. Lights fade.*)

SCENE FIVE

The fort. A courtroom. A large flag. MCLAUGHLIN *is on one side. The* GENERAL, DR. BEDDOES, DONNELLY, OTHERS. CATHERINE *is facing* MCLAUGHLIN. DONNELLY *raises a Bible. All rise.*

DONNELLY

The Army of the United States versus James McLaughlin, Agent, Indian Bureau, on charges of dereliction of duty, of aiding the enemy, and of profiting in the sale of Army goods, will continue. Mrs. Catherine Weldon, take the stand.

(*All sit.* CATHERINE *takes the stand, a small, low table like* MCLAUGHLIN*'s.*)

GENERAL

We'll continue where we left off yesterday.
We're glad you cooperated with our subpoena.
(*He shows her a letter.*)
This letter was intercepted by a trooper
who found it on a drunken Indian. Another brave
with their usual whisky courage.

CATHERINE

Where is Kicking Bear?

GENERAL

That's your main concern? Where is the Indian?
The Indian is where he belongs.

CATHERINE

You mean he's dead.

GENERAL

No, that is where he belongs, but at the moment
he's still with us. In the fort. In jail.
The lancer is a very decent man, from the East.
Until he learns our ways, ours and the Indians'.
You don't seem to care about the letter.
I do. I care a very great deal about this.
It's treasonable, it informs the enemy.

CATHERINE

Of what? There's nothing in the letter
of any martial value. It is personal.

GENERAL

Then you admit you wrote it.

CATHERINE

Yes. I may have. Yes,
I wrote to Sitting Bull, we are old friends.
My friendship remains. It is an older oath.

GENERAL

Why not use the post office? We've a post.

CATHERINE

And he's to do what, come and collect his mail?
And get his quota of flour from the agent,
and get roaring drunk and pass out in the street?

GENERAL (*Reading.*)
*If he had died on the Cannonball, I should be more
content; for then I would have buried him there and
remained near my Indians . . .*
(*He looks up.*)
Since when, Mrs. Weldon, did you acquire Indians?
(*He reads.*)

Now I am far from all my Dakota friends, and from
you, and my only child gone, too. Nothing left to me ...
(*He looks up.*)
"If he had died on the Cannonball." Who?
If who had died on the Cannonball, Mrs. Weldon?
Mrs. Weldon, if who had died on the Cannonball?

CATHERINE

My son. It says so later in the letter.
If my son had died on the Cannonball,
then I ...

GENERAL

Would have been happier?

CATHERINE

Happier?

DR. BEDDOES

It would have been more satisfactory.
That is the part that baffles me, you see,
that you could find some—what—some exaltation
in the exact geography of the boy's death.
Did you consider him a sacrifice to the Sioux?

CATHERINE

Sacrifice?

GENERAL

It's not a good sign, I've found,

from years of conducting tiring courts-martial,

when the defendant repeats the prosecution.

Yes. Happier. Your throat sounds dry. Do you want water?

CATHERINE

Water. No. Did you torture the Indian?

He'd have died rather than give up the letter.

GENERAL

He was drunk. Let Mrs. Weldon have water.

(*He reads.*)

And if your prayers to the Great Spirit are heard, pray to

give me a speedy death, that my heart may find peace.

(DONNELLY *gives* CATHERINE *water. She drinks.*)

CATHERINE

Thank you.

DONNELLY

My privilege, ma'am.

GENERAL

I'm interested in your attitude, Mrs. Weldon.

You're not a soldier. This is not a trial.

But this defies my command, threatens the fort.

CATHERINE

I'm a widowed woman. I was widowed young.
I asked Time questions. Time's answer is silence.
Since I was widowed, ghosts are more substantial,
the way things are in memory, than your hat,
and that is why I find no difficulty
at all in crossing the mute line, the boundary
that separates us from the Sioux,
for whom death is both pride and beauty
and the Great Spirit is a lifting wind.
Their victory will be in their defeat
because you, who are so terrified of death,
will be the ones to take them there.
You think, naturally, that I've given up.
Like no white woman with any sort of courage
should feel that I've caught the fever
of Indian despair, that worse, this is un-Christian,
but sometimes I feel exactly like them,
going through my ordinary chores:
that nothing can hurt me, that bullets
could go through my body, that
having accepted that secret happiness
that every tribe will share, sir,
I have never felt more alive.
Go and save your own souls, and not the Sioux's.
They've never tried to save yours.
That's the big difference.

GENERAL

Right, Mrs. Weldon.
You know Sitting Bull personally, Mrs. Weldon?

CATHERINE

I helped him to manage his business when he was
displayed in the circus by Colonel William Cody,
Buffalo Bill; all his dignity reduced
to a Roman spectacle, where he had to re-enact
the show business version of a howling, galloping savage
at the Little Big Horn. He ended up with no money.
Not after Colonel Cody's calculations of "expenses."
I painted his portrait.

DR. BEDDOES

Sitting Bull sat for you.

(*Laughter.*)

CATHERINE

You might say that.

DR. BEDDOES

I just did.

CATHERINE

Yes.
And whether it is a true likeness or not

(She unwraps the canvas.)
I have brought it with me to remind you gentlemen
of the great dignity and beauty of an old enemy.

(The GENERAL, *after checking with the others, nods.*
DONNELLY *unveils and displays the portrait.)*

DONNELLY

Looks a great deal like me grandma, sir.

GENERAL

Shut up, Sergeant Donnelly.

DONNELLY

She'd the constipation
something fierce. Thought I'd mention it, General.
'Tis an astonishing likeness if I may say so, ma'am.

GENERAL

Donnelly!

DONNELLY

Not another peep, sir.
(Pause.)
Only I don't like to see them treated as Christians when—
(He puts a finger to his own lips.)

CATHERINE

But they are Christians, Sergeant Donnelly. We made them.

First, we preach the Resurrection and the life,

of a Second Coming, of a pale-faced Messiah,

whom we have crucified so He can redeem us,

whom we must first murder to receive His pardon.

That must be baffling enough to those savages

who dare not presume to torture their gods.

When they go a little further, as all converts do,

of bringing heaven within their actual reach,

you turn and call them crazy. But they believed us.

They believed with us. Now what do you say?

You tell these converts that they believe too much.

That they exaggerate, they take belief too far.

That they misunderstood us or they're too immoderate.

When once you said that their doubt was indecent

and their gods were smoke.

(*Pause.*)

You made the Ghost Dance.

You forced Sitting Bull to this final hope.

I don't suppose you'll record any of this

as valuable testimony. You wanted more facts.

You look after the facts. I worry about faith.

Not only theirs, but my own now. I worry about madness.

Not theirs, but yours. About this civilisation

that you have brought to the Indians. A plague.

A pox. Sirs, a fever.

GENERAL
Thank you very much.
You may step down, Mrs. Weldon. Help her down.

(*Lights fade. Lights fade in immediately. The same.*
MCLAUGHLIN *in* CATHERINE's *place behind the box.*
CATHERINE *in his. Mime: Two horses may be either carved
or played by men with horses' heads. As* MCLAUGHLIN
speaks, holding up the letters in either hand, two couriers,
KICKING BEAR *and* BRANDON, *mount horses carved from
wood, stage left and stage right, carrying the two letters. Both
couriers, one Sioux, the other U.S. Army, have lances with
pennons. The Indian pony faces us, the Army horse is moving
in the opposite direction. Their riders mount and whip their
horses, hoisting their lances. Drums simulate the beat of their
hooves, stage left, stage right. The horses move at a gallop,
their riders, with different styles, bent over urgently.*)

MCLAUGHLIN
I sent a letter by a trooper, Lieutenant Brandon.
I begged him to gallop with utmost urgency.
(BRANDON *runs out carrying the letter, mounts the horse,
fixes his lance with its pennon as the drumming begins. Like
a relay race,* KICKING BEAR *is waiting near his mustang.*
DONNELLY, *in the court, carries one letter to the*
SECRETARY, *who receives it, reads it, as* MCLAUGHLIN
echoes its contents, with BRANDON *galloping,* KICKING

BEAR *waiting impatiently, pacing, soothing his horse.*

Drumming begins, then fades.)

To warn Sitting Bull on the Sioux Reservation

that the Army was mounting a huge offensive.

GENERAL

But this was the order that the Army sent you.

(*He reads.*)

Washington, December 1. McLaughlin, Agent. Standing Rock
—By direction of the Secretary, during the present Indian
troubles you are instructed that while you shall continue all
the business and carry into effect the educational and other
purposes of your agency, you will, as to all operations intended
to suppress any outbreak by force, cooperate with and obey the
orders of the military officers commanding on the Reservation
in your charge. R. V. Belt, Acting Commissioner. Correct?

(*Lights fade out, fade in immediately. The same.*)

Then there's this matter here about some blankets.

Is Paymaster Quint here, Sergeant Donnelly?

DONNELLY

Quint!

(QUINT *enters, timidly.*)

A tremblin' mouse of a man, sir.

He was only following orders, as I told him.

Shall I swear him in? Lift your claw, mouse.

(QUINT *goes to the stand.*)

Now put it on the Good Book and take the oath,
and quit that unmannerly tremblin'; go on.
Then tell them what you told me about the blankets.
(*He withdraws.*)

GENERAL

Do you solemnly swear—raise your right hand—
to speak the whole truth and nothing but the truth,
so help you God? Paymaster?

QUINT

That I do, sir.

DONNELLY

Quint. For the love of God, man, say what you know.

QUINT

Major McLaughlin come into stores one Wednesday
and ordered me to fetch him two, it was, blankets,
which I did promptly, sir. Then I requested
with great humility, sir, to sign a requisition
for the property, which he did. Except.
May I say this, sir?

DONNELLY

Christ, you might, Quint.

QUINT

With no ill will to you, Major McLaughlin, sir.
Except I'd say he falsified the intent.
I've the requisition here, sir.

(*He fumbles, finds it.*)

It's made out

as extra issue for a field excursion
with his Indian police, only that the blankets
are truly the property of the U.S. government,
that is, the Army, while he was with the bureau.
I later learnt from the Indian at the General Store
that the major carried them to Mrs. Weldon's trap,
and he watched him place them in the back of the trap.
It was only a matter of two blankets, sir,
'twasn't like a massacre or something.

DR. BEDDOES

It was a matter of departments, Corporal Quint.
It was a matter of having them for the Army hospital.
Can he step down?

GENERAL

You may step down, Quint.

(QUINT *steps down, relieved, smiling.*)

DONNELLY

You did good, Corporal Quint, extremely good.

QUINT

I didn't mince my words, did I, Donnelly? Oh, no.

DONNELLY

You've caught the fightin' spirit, Paymaster.

MCLAUGHLIN

Am I now on trial for two army blankets?

DR. BEDDOES

Or for aid and comfort to the enemy?

GENERAL

The blankets were Army property, Major McLaughlin.
They were not the property of the Indian Bureau,
since the bureau is under the Army's command.

MCLAUGHLIN

So I'm not only a traitor but a pilferer.

DR. BEDDOES

You took an oath.

MCLAUGHLIN

And what about your oath

as a doctor when you turned your back away

from the dying Indian girl they brought to you?

It's easy for all of us to hide behind an oath.

Of marriage, of fealty to a flag. Two blankets?

(*Lights fade out, fade in immediately. The same.*)

GENERAL

Lieutenant Brandon, will you read the verdict?

BRANDON (*Reading.*)

*You have been found guilty of consorting with the enemy to
the confusion and threatened defeat of your own country. You
heard the evidence of the court and have chosen to say nothing
in your own defence. However, because you are not a part of
the military but simply an Indian agent, the execution has
been lifted. But you will be stripped of your rank, your uniform, your responsibilities.*

(*He comes forward.*)

MCLAUGHLIN

Stand off, Brandon, I paid for this uniform.

A traitor is a liar. I am not a traitor.

I was trying to save the Indians by showing them

what terror lay ahead if they persisted.

GENERAL

All treachery is well intended; most traitors
explain their treachery as love of their country.
Well, I consider we have done you a great favour.
There's nothing to betray. You have no ranking now.
DISMISSED.

(*Lights fade.*)

SCENE SIX

The fort. MCLAUGHLIN *is in a cell. Undershirt, blanket,
leaning against his bunk.* MRS. MCLAUGHLIN, *his Indian
wife, is seated, in silence.* MCLAUGHLIN *says a few words in
Sioux. She doesn't reply. A* SENTRY *enters.*

SENTRY

You have a visitor, Major.

MCLAUGHLIN

Mister. Who?

(CATHERINE *enters. She sees* MRS. MCLAUGHLIN.)

CATHERINE

I beg your pardon.

MCLAUGHLIN

No. That's fine.

Except I can hardly ask you to come in.

CATHERINE

I'll come in. There's room.

(*To* SENTRY)

Can I go in?

(*The* SENTRY *nods, agreeing.* CATHERINE *bows to*
MRS. MCLAUGHLIN, *who bows, exits.*)

I am ashamed of my betraying you.

MCLAUGHLIN

I think I can redeem that shame. I've lost face, but
if I can do one action that was decisive, swift,
to show them that I have never betrayed the Army,
something so final that it would convince them
where my true sympathies lie, then my authority,
my respect would be restored. The thing was brought about
by Lucy's death. The Sioux may still be saved
by the sacrifice of Lucy. By Swift Running Deer.
There's no reason you should feel responsible.
Confined to quarters. Same damned thing as jail.
A sentry outside, and Donnelly peeping in.

Should have brought me a cake with a saw in it.
The longer I stay here, the worse it is for your friend.

CATHERINE

I can only hope they will restore your rank.

MCLAUGHLIN

Well, I don't know why you should hope for that.
To restore my rank is to restore my duty.
Which would put us back on opposite sides.
My duty is to prevent a Sioux uprising.
For their own sake. Once Colonel Cody
turned negotiations into another circus;
the Army has brought in extra troops and cannon,
so once I put my hand back on that Bible
and my rank is restored, I cannot betray
a second oath. You should hope the opposite.
You should hope they send me wandering on the Plains
with my squaw.

CATHERINE

I wouldn't want that.

MCLAUGHLIN

Spare me from the talented ones, the saved.
Spare me from those whose love is too stubborn
to see the consequences of such devotion.

Because I was one of them. I love you blindly,

the way you love that cunning old bastard still.

Perhaps I could collect all my Indian police.

They'd still obey me, out of uniform.

They're more devoted to me than to the Army.

If I could collect them. Get Little Eagle,

Hawk Man, Arm Strong. Bullhead. Afraid-of-Soldier.

They're good men. Sitting Bull's enemies.

If we could do it alone, without the Army.

Goddamn it, it can be done! For Lucy's sake.

But this time, Mrs. Weldon, you have to see my side.

CATHERINE

I'll try, Mr. McLaughlin. I owe you that much.

If what we do together is for Running Deer's sake.

MCLAUGHLIN

It is for the sake of the Sioux. Believe me.

It will stop this madness of the Ghost Dance.

(*Pause.*)

I loved you, Catherine Weldon,

Bright Hair Who Loved the Sioux.

Ah, why the past tense? I love you, for good.

CATHERINE

And I have loved you deeply, James McLaughlin.

(MCLAUGHLIN *moves away, turns his back.* CATHERINE
waits, exits. Lights fade.)

SCENE SEVEN

MCLAUGHLIN, *in civilian clothes, is testifying. Bare stage.*
MCLAUGHLIN *faces the audience.* GENERAL'S *voice
off, amplified.* CATHERINE *at the back.*

GENERAL'S VOICE
YOUR RECENT ACTIONS ARE TO BE COMMENDED.
YOUR RANK IS RESTORED. PROCEED. READ YOUR REPORT.

(MCLAUGHLIN *steps down to centre. He removes a report,
reads. During the reading of the report, distant cries and
gunfire faintly heard.*)

MCLAUGHLIN (*Reading.*)
Our Indian police rode into the camp before dawn.
We found Sitting Bull in the camp. He was in bed.
There were several Indians there from the Ghost Dance.
They believed, because of their magic shirts,
that no bullets could kill them. This we proceeded

to disprove. We seized Sitting Bull,

and some of the men tried to put him on a horse,

but several of my Indian police were backed up

against a wall by his followers. One of my men

held him around the waist, two others pinned his arms.

Then Sitting Bull shouted out something,

and then one of his followers shouted something,

then an Indian named Catch-the-Bear shot one of our men,

known as Bullhead. Bullhead, as he was falling,

shot Sitting Bull. It was at this point

that our police and the Sioux, the Ghost Dancers

who believed in their transparency, the potency

of their magic shirts, exchanged full fire

with our Indian police. Sitting Bull, we saw,

was wounded seven times. There were some dead:

these were his sons who died in the exchange.

(An Indian wail, long, slow, begins, then stops. Silence.)

GENERAL'S VOICE

WILL YOU PLEASE CONTINUE, MAJOR MCLAUGHLIN?

(CATHERINE *crosses behind* MCLAUGHLIN, *carrying*
blankets, which she hands to Paymaster QUINT, *exits.*)

MCLAUGHLIN (*Coughs, resumes.*)
These were his sons who died with him.

GENERAL'S VOICE

WE'RE LISTENING.

MCLAUGHLIN (*Resumes reading.*)

Crowfoot.

Jumping Bull.

Chase-Wounded, his grandson.

Catch-the-Bear.

Blackbird.

Spotted Horn Bull.

Brave Thunder.

(*Sioux death chant offstage.*)

GENERAL'S VOICE

KILLED.

MCLAUGHLIN

Sir. Yes, dead.

These are the Indian police who were killed.

GENERAL'S VOICE

DO WE NEED THE NAMES?

MCLAUGHLIN

They were my men, sir.

GENERAL'S VOICE

OF COURSE. READ THEM.

MCLAUGHLIN (*Faster.*)
Little Eagle, Hawk Man, Arm Strong . . .

GENERAL'S VOICE

NOT SO FAST, MAJOR.

MCLAUGHLIN

I was trying not to waste your time.
(*Slower, with tears.*)

Middle.
Afraid-of-Soldier.
Bullhead.
Shavehead.
(*The* GENERAL *emerges, with* BRANDON, *who carries*
a uniform. Pause.)
They spoke the Sioux language as they killed one another.
A language my wife has nearly forgotten.

GENERAL

The Army of the United States, Major McLaughlin,
will return your honours and your rank
because of the firm execution of your duty.
You have not only our apologies, sir,
but my admiration. You did very well,

and I know the shame you must have endured.
What has happened to that other fellow?
Kicking Bear. The Ghost Dancer.

MCLAUGHLIN

He's a free man, sir. A free Indian.
We let him out of the fort this morning.
Is that all, sir? My wife is outside.
And I'd like to say goodbye to Mrs. Weldon.

GENERAL

Let such duty be an example to you, Brandon.
I'm very proud of you, Jim. Very. Dismissed.

(*Lights fade.*)

SCENE EIGHT

The fort. DR. BEDDOES *passes, frock coat, cane, and shakes*
MCLAUGHLIN's *hand.* MRS. MCLAUGHLIN *waits some*
distance off. DR. BEDDOES *passes her, tips his hat.*
CATHERINE, *dressed for travel, appears on the street, her*
luggage carried by an Indian in Western clothes on a travois.
MCLAUGHLIN *comes up to* CATHERINE.

CATHERINE

I'm glad your rank was restored.

MCLAUGHLIN

So am I.

CATHERINE

So you go West, and I go back East, and between us,
this emptiness. The Land That Gives Back Nothing.
This silence they have left us with.

MCLAUGHLIN

Nothing between us.
Is that how you would put it, Catherine?

CATHERINE

Your wife's waiting in the wagon, Major McLaughlin.
No, I shouldn't say that. There was a great deal.
I hope you will make a good life out there.

(MCLAUGHLIN *takes her hand and kisses it. Silence.*)

MCLAUGHLIN

We got a place farther on.
I heard you were going back.

CATHERINE

As far as I can.

But we can't escape memory.

Every action has its ghost.

Every thought.

MCLAUGHLIN

Where will you be going now, then, Mrs. Weldon?

CATHERINE

I wish it were up in those white hills to join them.

MCLAUGHLIN

What would be the point of that? You'd freeze to death.

CATHERINE

Hallucinatory autumn, phantom spring,

the immaculate annihilation of deep winter,

to summer, sitting by the door, a distant cousin,

shucking cobs in a basin, the wife I was,

golden and ripe, growing up in the Dakotas,

with a brown firm husband, coming through the corn

with a brace of partridges over his shoulder,

to that girl, drowsing in midsummer's fire.

I know that he'll not come through the charred corn

with a brace of partridges over his shoulder;

I have arrived at that natural acceptance,

through nature, not through Progress. I can stand now
at the dead centre, at the heart of Time
where Time itself becomes a Ghost Dancer,
and everything that seemed surely insubstantial
returns, and that is the joy of the Ghost Dance,
that they, the Sioux, if they believe in nature,
must first die to return. Just like the seasons.
I was mad once. But this bright interval
is as lucid as a shaft of summer light
on a cabin's kitchen floor, when I was
what Lucy called me, "Bright Hair Who Loves Us."

MCLAUGHLIN

You will never accept my explanation.
But I'm not wickeder than any other man.

MRS. MCLAUGHLIN

James. Do you go now?

(MCLAUGHLIN *bows, exits with his wife.* CATHERINE
watches them leave. DONNELLY *comes up, holding the
portrait, gives it to* CATHERINE.)

CATHERINE

Well, the old battle whore is dead, isn't he, Sergeant?
Your best enemy's dead. What will preoccupy you now?
Look, all this country's yours from here to California.

DONNELLY

He should have worn the shirt. Still, now he's invisible.
You won't believe me, but I'm sorry he's gone, the old axe-
faced warrior. But then, with or without the sacred shirt,
we've all been promised a white sheet and a personal harp,
haven't we, and many of us believe it about the life to
come. But speakin' for meself, before that happens, I've
seen a real angel. I am looking at her now. Good luck
to you, Mrs. Weldon, ma'am. Well. That's all of it, then.

(*He turns, strides off, halts.*)

Oh! Thanks for all you taught Sarah.

CATHERINE

I simply taught her how to dance.

DONNELLY

Troopers!
Move off!

(*He turns, salutes. A bugle sound of cavalry moving off.*
He exits.)

TROOPERS (*Singing, drums and bugle.*)
Mine eyes have seen the glory
of the coming of the Lord;
He is trampling out the vintage
where the grapes of wrath
are stored . . .

(Snow begins to fall, thickly. KICKING BEAR, *in warrior costume, drunk, walks in the snow.* CONGREGATION *from church come out with bags of flour.* KICKING BEAR *collapses, frozen; flour is poured over him as the* CONGREGATION *withdraw.* INDIANS *mounted on toy horses appear through a scrim, galloping towards us.* CATHERINE *stands in light snow watching them; then* LUCY *appears in her Christian dress.)*

CATHERINE

And I can easily believe it, Swift Running Deer,
looking across to your life through a veil of snow,
that they will come back galloping, quiet as clouds,
to the Land That Gives Back Nothing, even to them.
I believe they are always there, always approaching,
like thunder without sound, on hooves of smoke,
those whom the land that gave them life belonged to—
Sitting Bull, Kicking Bear, and the leaves of the tribes,
the Blackfoot, the Sioux, the Ogalalas, the Cheyenne.

(They fade, approaching. CATHERINE WELDON
fades.)

December 5, 1995
Boston, Massachusetts